INDIA UN
EXPERIMENT

By GEORGE M. CHESNEY

LONDON
JOHN MURRAY, ALBEMARLE STREET
1918

INTRODUCTION

THE public has learned during the past autumn that further changes of the kind usually gilded by the name of reforms are to be introduced in the system of government which has hitherto prevailed in India. Wherever the momentum behind this experiment may lie, it is at any rate not to be accounted for by any stir of public opinion in the ruling country. The measures foreshadowed have not been discussed in Parliament, and, except for the transient gleam of interest imparted to them by Mr. Montagu's personal proceedings, have scarcely been noticed by the Press. By the general public, absorbed in so many other more pressing concerns, they have been totally unheeded. That alone should surely have been sufficient ground for postponing their introduction to a time more favourable for deliberation. But as things are done in these days, there is every reason to anticipate that the world will only hear of the matter after the decision has been arrived at, and when, as we shall be told, it is beyond the possibility of recall. As the Delhi Durbar was utilised to announce the change of capitals and redistribution of Provinces, in a way that closed the door to discussion or protest, so there is too much likelihood that the Montagu visit will be turned to account to spring upon India, and upon the owner, England, fundamental changes, upon which, it will be protested, once announced, there can be no going back. The combination of Secretary of State and Viceroy is evidently designed to invest their pronouncements with an appearance of authority that will put them beyond question. Who is to demur to the conclusions arrived at by the two chief personages, and only arrived at after a most patient hearing on the spot of the views of all classes ? To refuse assent to conclusions proclaimed under such sanction, we must be prepared to hear, is mere impracticability, for the reason that the disappointment of the expectations raised would increase the discontent the changes are intended to remove, and would even sanctify it. The contention may be difficult to answer then, but it does not remove the objections to the manœuvring by which the situation will have been created. The preliminary consultation

of the affected interests which has been going
on in India during the winter can only be a
matter of form, for the main issue was pre-
determined from the day that Mr. Montagu,
in August, announced his intention of going
to India to prepare the way for the change of
policy for which he took the name of the
Cabinet. If his ideas were to change under
contact with local opinion, could he avow it
in face of the undertaking he had given ?
The reader will be able to form his own
opinion of the probability of such a conversion.
Taking it for granted, then, that the cause
has been prejudged, the object of this work
is to set forth as intelligibly as may be to the
British public, which, after all, is an interested
party to the case, the probable character of
these changes, their probable effects and
ultimate bearings. The difficulty of the task
lies in the obscurity in which the plans of the
promoters are shrouded. After the fashion
in which " popular " government works, the
secret will be carefully kept until the moment
when the lid comes off and the public is
bidden to swallow the stew with the best face
it can, for nothing else will it get. To keep
the world carefully in the dark while the
selected project is maturing, to plead high

reasons of State for refusing all information during the preparatory stages, to dismiss all criticism as ill-informed and premature, and finally, when the result is produced, to tell dissentients "it is too late now; you should have objected sooner"—this is the simple mode of procedure by which the democratic Behemoth is nose-ringed and brought to follow wheresoever his leaders may be willed to draw him, while with a few adroit pats on the flanks they persuade him to believe that he is taking his own way.

NOTE

*" Il me semble que le bonheur de cette nation
n'est point fait comme celui des autres. . . .
Voilà qui s'est fait un gouvernement unique dans
lequel on a conservé tout ce que la monarchie a
d'utile et tout ce que une république a de néces-
saire. . . . Je la vois seulement embarrassée de
l'Amerique septentrionale qu'elle a conquise à un
bout de l'univers, et des plus belles provinces de
l'Inde subjugées à l'autre bout. Comment portera-
t-elle ces deux fardeaux de sa felicité ?"*

VOLTAIRE: *Eloge de la Raison.*

CONTENTS

INDIA UNDER EXPERIMENT

CHAPTER I

THE REWARD OF LOYALTY

No one sufficiently interested in the subject to be at the trouble of opening these pages will be unaware that the young years of the present century have been a period of continual activity in the extension of political advancement in India. He is also likely to have been struck by the reflection that the more he hears of reforms the worse the accounts he gets of political discontent. The nature of the changes that have been going on will have to be considered more particularly later. Broadly they fall under three heads: The extension of representative institutions of the Parliamentary type in the form of the Legislative Councils; the extended employment of Natives of India in the public service, which is the prime feature in Indian polity; and the extension of local self-government through the fostering of Municipalities and District Boards. This third branch of the subject, though it represents a most useful and promising experiment, hardly comes into the field of controversy, and to avoid loading the discussion may be left aside here. The promotion of representative institutions and the increased employment of Indian agency in the Public Service, though the two things have no necessary connection, have been going on hand in hand. Both lines of advance have been followed in the idea that they would be equally acceptable to the political class whom it was desired to conciliate, and each concession has generally come at the tail of some outburst of agitation for which it is going to be a sedative, but promptly acts in practice as a fresh irritant. Judging by results, the plan of propitiation has proved itself, in this regard, a signal failure. Whatever the explanation, the fact is incontestable that Indian discontent first assumed a serious form simultaneously with its coming to knowledge that Lord Morley was engaged on preparing a great scheme of " reforms "; and now, since it has come to be understood that Mr. Montagu was contemplating another instalment going far beyond the achievements of his predecessor, the differences and animosities excited by the prospect have risen to a pitch unknown hitherto.

What is the reason for the resumption in such dire haste of a process which has such an unfortunate record ? The war, with all the dislocations it is producing in the normal course of civil life, its inroads upon individual liberty, even upon freedom of discussion, constitutes surely reason sufficient for putting off large constitutional changes to a better day. But in the mouth of those who are pressing these changes the war becomes another argument for precipitancy. India requires to be rewarded for her splendid, her astonishing loyalty in the war; and this loyalty of Native Chiefs, of Gurkhas, Pathans, Dogras, Sikhs, Jats, of transport-drivers and coolies, is to be repaid by political concessions to classes with whom these have little more in common than with the Bolsheviks. In addition to its ludicrous inaptness, the compensation argument carries within itself the destructive assumption that if it is not swiftly and adequately recognised this magnificent loyalty will turn to something less pleasant. Moreover, the language used on the subject implies that the sentiment is something un-

looked for, a recent growth, the fruit, you
are invited to imagine, of the Morley-Minto
reforms. This insinuation does the grossest
wrong to the spirit of the country. As for
the Native Chiefs, people generally do not
realise all that they have done and given up
in the cause of the Empire since, forty years
ago, at the instance of Lord Beaconsfield,
Queen Victoria was proclaimed as their Queen-
Empress. Not only have they volunteered
to send their troops to every military service
that offered, but they have consented—a far
harder matter to them—to the abolition of
transit duties in their States, to the abolition
of their own mints, to the abolition of their
own armies. The transit duties are to the
Oriental mind the first and most natural source
of revenue; the local mint was an attribute of
royalty, the local army was another. It is
impossible for us to realise what sacrifices the
Chiefs must have made of their sentiments in
giving up these marks of sovereignty, but one
after another they were persuaded that the
surrender of these individual prerogatives
would make for the general welfare of the
country, and they complied. They made no
grievance of the matter, they asked for no
reward; it was only when an ill-judged sugges

tion was put forward for converting their personal voluntary contributions to the Imperial Service scheme into a fixed levy that they showed signs that their patience was being tried. It was a hard thing for a Native Ruler to give up his own army of his own retainers, even if the army was nothing more than a squadron of "looty-wallah" horse with a banner and a kettle-drum. An Imperial Service Company of khaki-clad Pioneers or a Transport Train unit is not at all the same thing in sentiment, and, moreover, requires regular payment. Still, it represents a free-will offering on the part of the State, whereas to impose a contribution as part of a universal rule would have destroyed all the grace and the chivalry of the idea. Happily, circumstances interfered with the realisation of the plan, and under the tactful, sympathetic working of the handful of picked Military Officers to whom the general superintendence of the Imperial Service Scheme has been entrusted, the system, as it has grown to manhood, has completely gained the affections of the Chiefs themselves. But to speak of the loyalty of this class is in truth superfluous, when almost every year sees evidence of it in their liberality towards projects started by the

Government for the benefit of the country at large, in many of which, Imperial Institutes, Memorial Halls at Calcutta, and the like, they can only have the remotest personal interest. The danger is, in fact, that their readiness in giving may lend itself to abuse; and on one occasion at least it was only the outspoken protests of the Anglo-Indian Press that prevented their merciless exploitation for the happy thought of an impetuous Viceroy.

Next in the catalogue of services which call for reward (in the shape of representative institutions and increased Government employment for English-speaking discontent) comes the war-work of the Indian Army. That, too, is commonly spoken of as if it were something beyond anticipation and experience—something, after all, it would seem, to the credit of Lord Morley, and an encouragement to persevere in his footsteps. Such language is as absurdly wide of the mark as the impressions on which it rests. The Indian Army has behaved precisely as would have been expected of it. There have been some exceptions to the general rule, it is true—we cannot afford to forget the savage mutiny at Singapore—and there have been uncomfortable "incidents " on a comparatively small scale in various Indian cantonments, but these combined do not weigh a grain against the immense mass of general loyalty.

But who looked for anything but loyalty from the Indian Army ?   To anyone who has seen the splendid collection of manhood which is represented by the officers of any good Native regiment the supposal of a bad spirit is preposterous.   No doubt the Indian soldier is inclined to dislike leaving his own land, no doubt the idea of service against Europeans is unwelcome to him; still more, perhaps, the idea of service against his co-religionists.   But these considerations have not counted in times when they had greater weight.   The year 1914 was not exactly the first occasion of a call for service beyond seas.   In 1801 Lord Wellesley despatched a force from Bombay to co-operate with the British operations in Egypt.   A decade later the first Lord Minto sent out the expeditions which took Mauritius from the French and Java from the Dutch.   In 1824 came the war with Burma, then an unknown country beyond seas reputed to be held by mighty men of valour.   To come to more recent times, in 1877 Indian regiments embarked for Malta, enthusiastic at the

prospect of a Russian war to follow, and in
1882 went just as readily to Egypt to fight
against Arabi Pasha. It would be idle to go
to instances such as the Afghan and trans-
frontier wars, for the sepoys with whom the
Company's forces began enlisted with the
knowledge that their enemies would be their
own countrymen and co-religionists. Plassey
was won by a force of Madrassi sepoys alongside with part of the 39th Foot. The French
were driven from Southern India by a force in
which Native regiments from the Bengal side
figured conspicuously. Fidelity to the service
first is a sentiment that runs strong in the
Indian nature, and possibly the highest
exemplification of it is in the case of the
humble police-constable, who goes out to
arrest a dangerous outlaw or a wealthy land-
owner without consideration of whether his
man is a Mahomedan or a Hindu. Remu-
nerated at the rate of a domestic scullion,
this humble servant of the State has some of
the failings natural to his circumstances, but
his enemies seldom complain that he fails out
of scruples for the caste or creed of offenders.
At any rate, there is a high spirit of duty and
solidarity prevailing through this civil army,
which rests ultimately, like that of the army

proper, on common confidence in its British officers. The only question, in fact, that could arise in regard to the loyalty of the army was whether it might not have been unfixed to some extent by the intrigues of the agitators, who, not only after the outbreak of the war, but for some years before, had notoriously been making very persistent attempts to get hold of the soldiers. The few scattered cases of misconduct that did occur were due to this influence. But the minute outcrop of the mischief in comparison with the efforts made to implant it is in reality a striking sign of how little influence this political class possesses with the mass of the people.

As for these masses, it was the Duke of Wellington, then Colonel Wellesley, who wrote of them that they are the only real political philosophers in the sense of not caring who their governors may be. The bulk of the population still consists of 80 per cent. of peasants, living their own lives in their own villages, the chief change lying in their horizons having been enlarged by the railway, which, much more than the school, has been the general educator. It would be absurd to look in such a population for any reasoned loyalty to a foreign Government, and doubly absurd to suppose that they have any appreciation of the changes that have come about within that Government between 1858 and 1918.   What they ask of a Government is that it shall be cheap, that it shall let them alone as much as possible—seeing that throughout the Eastern world the contact of minor officials always means oppression—and that it shall guarantee even-handed justice.   If, in addition, it helps them over famine and affords them reasonable protection against the land-owner and the usurer, their political requirements are tolerably satisfied.   No one would pretend that finality has been or will be reached in these respects; but the peasant is much less conscious than his rulers of the short-comings of the system.   It would be foolishness for any one person — even though a foreigner and a non-official—to formulate on his own account any dictum on the general state of mind of that vast population; but it may be said that all the available evidence is that the feeling of the people towards their governors was never so good as in 1914.   The period 1896-1910 was notable for an un-paralleled recurrence of famines, any one of which would have formerly represented a hideous total of mortality and suffering; and unquestionably in many parts of the afflicted Provinces a comprehension of what was being done for them by Government, brought home by personal touch with the officers working in their midst, did penetrate the stolid mind of the villagers. Their minds should have also been affected to some extent by experience of the long-continued fight that the Government has been making against plague, though at first its efforts to protect them were an additional terror. The growth of the Co-operative Village Banking system, a departure launched and developed by the unsympathetic British official entirely on his own motion, as he alone understood the burden of rural debt, has undoubtedly contributed to good feeling; and, above all, there was the incident of the King's Coronation Durbar, which beyond any question elicited a manifestation of feeling so universal and spontaneous that it took by surprise those who knew the country best. Allowing for the ease with which an appearance of public opinion can be manufactured in a population where none exists, the stir of delight and gratification which went through India on the occasion of the King's visit was unquestionably genuine, and, allowing for the

strange way in which the sentiment of Indians
attaches itself to the Ruler in virtue of his
office—so that he whom we should call a bad
Raja does not appear to be less popular
personally than a model one—could not have
been what it was if the rule of which His
Majesty was the embodiment had been un-
acceptable to the masses.

One may repeat, therefore, that the general
sentiment of India was probably, in its passive
way, never better affected towards the British
connection than at the date when the war
broke out.   But in any case how should we
have expected the people to behave ?   Did we
suppose that they would declare for the
Germans ?   In this respect there was abundant
guidance from the past.   Not one in a thousand peasants had up to that moment ever
heard of the Germans; but a good deal had
undoubtedly been heard of the Russians by
the time that they had worked their way to
the environs of Herat.   From the Caspian to
Calcutta there is a continuous highway of
communication, and from the day when the
Emperor Paul, in 1801, formed the first scheme
for a Russian invasion, the Indian ear had
become sensitive to echoes of the tramp of

approaching hosts in the north-west. Louder
continually grew the sound as they came
pushing on through the Turkoman country,
absorbed Khiva, Bokhara, and Merv, until at
last it broke into a crash with the collision at
Panjdeh in 1885. All these years India had
been invaded each winter by the caravans of
Afghan merchants, easy-going, free-spoken
giants with rosy cheeks and long curls, who
penetrate every corner of the country down
to Tuticorin; inveterate traders and wanderers
who did not break off their annual rounds even
during the Mutiny. When these strangers
lit their fires in the market-town at evening
their talk would be of the " Russ," and doubt-
less they did not spare the imaginations of the
country-folk as to the coming terror. Towards
the end of the century a vague presentiment
of a great collision impending must have been
abroad everywhere; but there was certainly
no sign of any disposition in favour of the
Russians. What conceivable inducement,
then, should the Indians have had for attach-
ing themselves to Germany, who in the
interior of the country, if known at all, was
only known in the person of a trader in some
despised *métier*—a buyer of bones, hides,
bristles, or a commercial traveller pushing

cutlery made up to resemble that of Sheffield ?
The German missionary no doubt abused his
position to the utmost of his capacity, but
would not be much better placed for mischief. In fact, the German inability to
influence coloured races has been shown
by their failure in Africa, where they had
a long-established footing to begin with.
If they could have raised the natives against
us there in the east and west, they would not
have needed to trouble with India. It is not,
of course, to be denied that they did establish
relations to a certain extent with the Hindus
in North America and with the agitators in
Bengal. But it is these who represent the
advanced wing of the agitation which it is
now proposed to propitiate, and who form the
only notable exception to the general loyalty.

In conclusion, it is totally misleading to
speak of Indian loyalty, Indian discontent,
Indian wants and wishes, and so forth, when
the attitude and feelings in question vary
totally in different Provinces. These expres-
sions are cultivated sedulously by the politicals
for the sake of producing an artificial appearance of unity, and have to be used sometimes
for the sake of brevity, but the impression

they convey is a perversion of the reality.
One great Province, for example, since the
war began has shown, let us say, an uncertainty
of disposition which has been a constant
anxiety to the Government; while another
has exhibited a shining example of the opposite
disposition, that would deserve recognition
had it been forthcoming from any part of
the Empire. The Punjab since the outbreak
of the war has given proof of a spirit not
inferior to that of 1857, when it saved India
for Britain. This Province, with a population of less than twenty millions, was furnishing when the war began about 55 per cent. of
the strength of the entire Indian Army.
Instead of considering this remarkable contribution sufficient, the people of the Punjab
treated the outbreak of war as a call to themselves, just as if they had been Australians
or Canadians. Many hardy tribes, men with
all the makings of soldiers, but who had not
been accustomed, like the Sikhs, to the practice of enlistment, now came forward to
answer the appeal in swarms. Recruiting
has flourished ever since. The total contribution of the Province up to the beginning of
November last was 220,000 men, of whom
four-fifths were combatants. In the last

three months of this period the recruits numbered 39,000, more than the total for the whole of the rest of India. The only slackening to be feared is from the shrinkage of the population of military age. That amounts to about four millions, including the Punjab Native States, and even in the Punjab different parts of the Province differ. In one of the five Divisions the people show comparatively little bent for military service, with the result that the call falls all the more heavily on the others. What the strain involves which the willing population takes on itself is shown by the figures for the Rawul Pindi Division, the head centre of supply for the army. They are well worth a moment's attention. In the first period of the war, to the end of March, 1915, 45,000 recruits were enlisted altogether in India; of these, the Rawul Pindi Division furnished 11,000. By the end of October last its contribution had amounted to 75,000, of whom five-sixths were combatants, this, added to the number of men already serving in the ranks when the war broke out, bringing the total to over 100,000 men from a single portion of a single Province. This meant, said the Lieutenant-Governor, Sir M. O'Dwyer, in a local Durbar, that one man in every six of fighting age is serving in the defence of the

Empire. Of one tehsil of the Division, the Deputy-Commissioner wrote: " It has become normal for a boy on reaching maturity—if not before—to go off and enlist. A number of villages in this ilaqua contain only old men, boys, and invalids !" In the Rawul Pindi Division the people are chiefly Punjabi Mahomedans, but in the Sikh districts the spirit has been equally fine. In the Sikh State of Jhind, whose people are only in a secondary sense subjects of the Empire, out of a total of 49,000 of military age, one man out of every seven has gone into the British service; and the neighbour States of Patiala and Nabha show scarcely less striking results. Well may this be called "magnificent" loyalty, which shows the people voluntarily undertaking a burden equal to anything that could have been imposed on them by any system of conscription, had that principle been conceivable. But the unblushing appropriation of the loyalty of Northern India as a reason for rewarding Provinces which practically have not furnished a man to the Empire's cause with political boons which would ultimately place the military classes under the power of Bengalis and Madrassis is an extravagance that can only pass as long as the situation is not understood.

CHAPTER II

THE REWARD OF DISAFFECTION

IF the foregoing brief survey of the condition
of things as they stand among the classes who
have been contributing to the war disposes of
the idea that the motive of political reforms
can be in the necessity of rewarding them,
since the scheme does not benefit them at all,
it must needs be that the purpose behind the
project is that of conciliating the discontented.
As a loose description of this class, it might
be said to consist of those who have been educated at the schools and colleges, which for
practical purposes are all under the superintendence of the Government Department
of Public Instruction.   It would be very
wrong to imply that all the educated are discontented.   There are large numbers of them,
especially among the considerable body
employed in the public services, who are just
the contrary, thoroughly loyal, but these are
not heard of.

On the other hand, it may be truly said

that all the discontented are educated. Even the crudest youth who is got hold of to fling the bomb or fire the revolver is invariably found to have received some tincture of education at a school before he was fit for the promptings of the anarchist. In passing, it may be noticed that the revelations produced in recent criminal trials of the moral state of the schools where some of these anarchist crimes have been hatched have been so frightful that they must have raised an outcry in England if it were possible that the public here should be effectively responsible for what happens in India. One of the worst corrupters of youth, who has paid the final penalty, was an ex-teacher at a missionary college, a man who had been well liked and trusted by his English colleagues. But of course all the discontented are not anarchists. At the other end of the line is the urbane gentleman who brings forward resolutions in his Legislative Council which he knows well are in no danger of passing, because it is pleasant to feel oneself in the van of progress, and also because a little opposition does one no harm with Government, being often the shortest road to a C.I.E. But one way or another, be it moderate or extremist, fictitious

or fanatical, there is no question of the exist
ence of a body of opposition in the country
which alone has the ear of the outside world
and which is constantly increasing in volume
in defiance of every palliative hitherto devised
by the rulers. The situation is a serious one
as everyone will acknowledge who realises
that to the Government, on whom all this
criticism and complaint constantly drips
there is no alternative. In the second place
in spite of the vast size of India, of all the
radical differences between the different
components of the population, the opposition
has no checks within itself. There is no
discrimination of right, left, or centre.
Temporary personal differences between
leaders, such as broke up the National Congress at Surat, are of no consequence whatever
in the long run. The only one outstanding
difference of interests among the agitators
was merged when the Moslem League last
year formally announced its amalgamation
with the Hindu Congress. Henceforth whatever is is wrong—and all the complaint falls on
the head of the Government. But between
an irremovable Government and an un-
divided, implacable Opposition, allowed the
freest opportunities of expression, the situa-

tion must eventually grow serious. The question now, from the political point of view, is whether the concessions in contemplation are likely to act as a remedy.

It must be allowed that the argument from experience is not encouraging. Whatever view may be taken of the different measures that have been introduced during the last forty years with the object of popularising the Government, it is a simple matter of fact that, severally and in the sum, they have had no other effect than that of increasing the volume and embittering the tone of the opposition. To attempt to analyse the causes of this anomalous manifestation would be a long task, but of the fact itself there can be no more question than of the deepened discontent of Ireland since the passage of the Home Rule. Lord Ripon's popular policy of the early eighties was speedily followed by an agitation that led to the formation of the National Congress, whose whole tone has been more or less vehement condemnation of the existing order of things.

Occasionally a conciliatory orator may counsel patience till the transient darkness of the present age has dissolved into the glories of a state in accordance with Indian

3

aspirations; but this is the utmost. I can never remember having read a Congress speech which was a frank, reasoned upholding of the British administration—not because Indians, as will be found in private conversation, are not alive to its merits, but because such a line would expose the speaker to unmeasured obloquy in the Indian Press. Lord Lansdowne enlarged the Legislative Councils, introducing into their composition the new element of a certain proportion of non-official members to be nominated by various public bodies and interests, such as the Chambers of Commerce, the Universities, and the big landholders' associations. This Bill of 1892 also made provision for the regular discussion of Budgets, imperial and provincial. Hitherto, as the status of the Councils had been merely that of committees engaged upon the details of legislation, even the Imperial Budget could not be discussed unless it involved the passing of some Bill. So if there was no new tax or duty requiring to be imposed or abolished, the Indian Chancellor of the Exchequer simply read his statement, and financial discussion, with all that general ventilation of public affairs that comes in its train, was postponed for another year. It is easy to judge, there-

fore, that Lord Lansdowne's measure was in
reality a very important departure in the
direction of giving Indian public opinion a
voice and influence in Government affairs.
But there was nothing in it to appeal to the
school which set the tone of the National
Congress, and the opposition never ceased to
grow in acerbity. Four years later the
country came to be faced with a rising of the
hill tribes all round the North-west Frontier
under some strange general stirring of antagonism towards their unaggressive neighbour,
and Lord Elgin's Government felt obliged, in
the interests of security, to put another rein
upon the weak bridle holding the Native
Press.

In Lord Curzon's day agitation was kept
in abeyance outwardly by the belief that the
Government was in strong hands, but towards
the latter part of his Viceroyalty two measures
were introduced which produced violent
searchings of heart—the reform of University
education and the partition of Bengal. The
latter was a provincial grievance merely, and
to this day it is a matter of doubt how far the
loud-voiced agitation which burst out over
the subject was a genuine one or a case of a
pretext seized by a faction on the look-out for

a good grievance. At any rate, the complaint did not come from the districts that were severed off by the partition, but from the unaffected half whose centre was Calcutta. It is difficult to believe a change which touched no man in any material respect whatsoever could have been a lasting trouble, and in any case it is flattering to British rule that a territory which represents nothing more than a series of administrative arrangements should have come to acquire the sanctity of a motherland. But though Lord Morley would not cancel the partition, he was much impressed by the surface vehemence of the agitation, and thus the demonstrations which culminated in the impressive crowning of Mr. Surendranath Bannerjee as Sovereign of Bengal were among the reasons that brought him up to the conviction that the Government must be popularised according to British political recipes.

The first result was most unpromising; it was no sooner understood that the Secretary of State and the Viceroy were projecting an extensive scheme of "reforms" than agitation began to assume a new and darker shade. From meetings on the Calcutta maidan, addressed in a turgid imitation · of classical British exemplars, it was a long but swift transition to that of the orators who now began to inflame audiences of a different character in Upper India. The Government was obliged to act in self-defence, and not too soon. The excitement aroused by the idea of impending reforms spread from the Punjab even to Madras, and when it led to rioting in the somnolent far south of that tranquil Province it was evident that the right of public speaking must be placed under restriction. Measures were adopted to that end, but to get rid of the heads of the disturbance another means was adopted. There was a Regulation still in existence that empowered the Government to arrest an inconvenient person in British India, and deport or intern him at its pleasure. Passed in 1818, at a time when the British Raj was still confronted by powerful independent elements in the country, it was intended to provide a means for dealing with people of the class of descendants of the Peshwa (such as Nana Sahib, if he had shown his hand earlier, instead of posing as an Anglophil), emissaries from the Courts of Lucknow or Delhi, the Sikh Rani Jindhan, and the like.

Now this antique ordinance was brought out by a Radical Secretary of State to be employed against ordinary subjects of the Government for an ordinary class of offence, and a very useful instrument it was found, to judge by the employment made of it.

As the enthusiasm created by the prospect of political reform extended, further encroachments upon the established course of judicial procedure followed. The various secret conspiracies aimed at the overthrow of the Government which in due time succeeded the inflammatory public meeting quite outran the capacity of the statutory law courts, with their cumbrous system, which gives every serious criminal case the chance of expanding over three trials. It was impossible to deal with batches of eighty or ninety accused on a scheme of procedure which would have merely made the judgment of the Sessions Court, after a three or four months' investigation, the preliminary to a retrial in the High Court. A new emergency jurisdiction had therefore to be created in the shape of Special Tribunals of three Judges appointed *ad hoc*, who, working under simplified rules as to the admission and record of evidence and in the spirit of justice rather than legality, have managed to get through their work, which is exempt from the right of appeal.

The justice which these Special Tribunals have administered has been very little criticised. Nevertheless, they are not institutions that a constitutionalist can regard with a friendly eye, even if he may reluctantly admit their necessity. But before the large-scale conspiracy came upon the scene, the era of anarchist outrage had intervened. The bomb first burst on the Indian world in the murder of two English ladies at a quiet mofussil station by an explosion intended for a Civilian Judge who had incurred the resentment of the Nationalists. Then followed a series of outrages of the same general type, which culminated with the attempt on the life of the Viceroy, Lord Hardinge, as he was heading a State procession through Delhi. All the crimes, or attempted crimes, of this period have a common resemblance in having been perpetrated by young men, sometimes not out of boyhood; and on this account they were sometimes dismissed as the work of irresponsible students. But it is now well known that behind each of the actual criminals was a band of instigators, reaching back to the headquarters of the society, who spent perhaps months in working their intended agent up to the proper frame of mind. Moreover, it has to be remembered that for one youth found willing and trustworthy for the actual execution of an outrage, scores were probably sounded and tampered with, so the spread of the poison cannot be judged by the number of those brought to the dock. In fact, the really serious feature about the anarchist propaganda is not the amount of crime that has been committed, but the fact that the whole student world, the manhood of the coming generation, has become familiarised with the doctrine that the cause of the country may be promoted by crime, and that the vilest crimes become sanctified when committed for that cause.

Next to adopting such a creed himself, the worst thing that can happen to a young man is that he should know that it is held by many about him. In the first instance, the men to be initiated would be told that they had the means of freeing the country in their hands if they would but devote themselves. The English officials were few—only three or four to each district—and a combined scheme of assassinations would therefore soon bring foreign rule to an end. It was this vein of purpose that ran through the outcrop of murders and attempts at murders which occurred sporadically from Dacca in Eastern Bengal to South Kensington, and in which, for some obscure reason, in practically every instance the victim marked down was known for his special sympathy with the people of the country, as, for instance, Sir Curzon Wylie; Mr. Jackson, the collector of Nassick; Sir Andrew Fraser, the Lieutenant-Governor of Bengal; and Lord Hardinge himself. Presumably the idea was that if a beginning was made with notably popular characters, the policy of ruthlessness would find no scruples to check its momentum afterwards.

After a year or two of this, however, the plan of campaign underwent a remarkable change of direction. The organisers, for whatever reason, had come to feel that success did not lie in the extermination of the British official, and the next effort was turned upon their own countrymen, the Native officers of the Police. Unlike the first movement, the new departure was confined almost entirely to Bengal. There any Police officer who had shown himself vigilant and capable in the detection of political crime soon came to know that he carried his life in his hand. The series of assassinations of investigating officers which now set in were marked by the utmost audacity, several of these crimes being committed in crowded thoroughfares in Calcutta, and one of them within the precincts, of the High Court itself. The object was to terrorise the intelligence branch of the Police as a preparative against the new form of activity that was in contemplation. Suddenly the public began to hear of burglaries in the country districts, crimes of a new type in which the ordinary housebreaker was replaced by gangs of youths of the middle class, armed with revolvers and after a fashion disciplined, who posted sentries to secure the approaches while others entered the house to secure the owner's horde and rifle his zenana. Unless report errs grossly, the leaders in these enterprises were generally rural schoolmasters. The proceeds of these burglaries, which were often large, were generally paid into the central crimes fund, and it appears to have been this association which after the outbreak of the war got into touch with German agents in the Straits and Sumatra, and, in concert with them, devised a wild scheme for an insurrection, which seems to have been timed to come off in the midwinter of 1915-1916, and naturally came to nothing. This Neo-Thuggism, or "political criminality" as it was officially labelled, appears to have been practically confined to Bengal, where it throve on the weakness of the provincial administration.

· The only other element in the population who can be suspected of any dealings with the Germans were the Indian out-residents in the States, especially among their haunts along the Pacific Coast. For some reason the Hindu mind goes bad with special rapidity in the pleasant climate of California, and the colony at San Francisco, under the leadership of the notorious Hurdyal—an Oxonian like his counterpart Mr. Krishnavarma of Paris—had become little better than a murder school. Unfortunately, their tenets had spread to men of a different class, chiefly Sikhs, who had come to frequenting British Columbia because of the demand for labour. When the local Government, becoming aware of the undesirable spirit at work among this class, had prohibited Asiatic immigration, the leaders determined to see whether an entry could not be forced. They chartered a vessel, took up Sikh immigrants from the Straits, China, and Japan, and eventually appeared at Vancouver demanding an entry. The patience of the local authorities averted a collision, and the *Komagata Maru* slowly made her way back to Calcutta, freighted with as ill-minded a set of men as has assembled on one deck since the days of piracy. Strangely, they were allowed to land with their arms, of which they promptly availed themselves at the railway-station where they were told to entrain, a serious conflict ensuing, with a considerable bill of casualties. After this they were confidingly sent off to their homes in the Punjab, where the forward spirits at once set about attempting to organise a general insurrection, which was to have commenced with the seizing of local treasuries and gone on to the capture of arms and military stores. But they had chosen the wrong place; the general loyalty and sense of the Punjab countryside was too pronounced to give them any real chance of success and the intended revolt collapsed, after having been carried far enough to show how clearly the rural people were not for incendiary politics.

No survey of the recent state of India would have been adequate without reference to this unpleasant subject. Different people will no doubt read its importance differently. There are optimists who are able to regard violence of this kind as a mere speck on the mirror; there are others who look upon it as a putrid fungus requiring summary eradication. Without attempting to hold the balance, it may be suggested that the serious feature is the little condemnation that " political " crime receives from public opinion. It was left to the Punjab peasantry to produce an effective opposition to the movement brought over in the *Komagata Maru*. The Press and the platform will deprecate an outrage, when it has to be noticed, in the correct language imposed on men claiming to share the standards of civilisation; but when the State is obliged to take some measure for dealing with the mischief, an extension of Police powers, restrictions on public meetings, or an amendment of the Press regulations, then the opposition takes a different language. The mild disapproval of crime or violence disappears in the hot indignation excited by the precautions adopted against its spread, with their infringement of the liberties of the citizen. The " moderate " legislative councillor deplores the necessity of the measure in his Council, and warns the Government of the grave consequences he foresees from repression; the vernacular Press, always in a fury, assumes an extra vehemence, often descending into bathos as the writers proceed to enlarge on the unhappy future of the people now that their last safeguards have been taken away. In explanation of the practically unvarying hostility of all the criticism that the Government encounters from outside, which has become such an unfortunate feature of the situation in India, the prime cause to be taken into account is the attitude of journalism. The audacious juxtaposition of a free Press and an absolute Government was due to Metcalfe's repeal of the existing Press regulations when he was officiating as Governor-General in 1836. The act has been often in later years absurdly ascribed to his credit on grounds that could not have occurred to him. There was no Native Press in existence in his day, and the papers he was concerned with were a few European journals in Calcutta, conducted by men who deserved little respect on their own account, but who are still remembered for the severities with which they were treated. Metcalfe could hardly foresee the day when a news-sheet of local personalities, whose circulation trickled perhaps as far as Murshidabad and Midnapore, would become a live force in the country, and he aimed merely at putting an end to the unedifying squabbles to which the clash between the Government and a few struggling editors was constantly giving rise. As far as his immediate object was concerned, the Liberal policy was completely successful. In the course of a few years' time the old journalism was replaced by publications like the *Friend of India* and the *Calcutta Review*, a newspaper and a magazine that would have been a credit to any community.

But the result was that when education had spread, when railway communication had been introduced and extended, the Native Press, when it came into being, found itself in possession of a clear field, of which it soon began to take advantage. People who elaborately ascribe every symptom of discontent to some pre-existent sense of injury or repression will find it difficult to make out that explanation here. The Press, to begin with, was mostly, outside the Presidency towns entirely, in the hands of persons of small estimation. They turned to opposition often by way of recommending themselves to the notice of Government for an appointment, sometimes by way of exploiting the opportunities opened to the profession by the excessive tenderness of their countrymen in the matter of blackmail. Moreover, the Indian Press, to begin with, was entirely in Hindu hands, and the Hindu is a determined pessimist. Like the Hebrew of old, he looks back to a golden past, when the fair land and large belonged exclusively to his own people, and fastens his ideas on a revival of this age of splendour in the future; but in the meantime the world is full of darkness and unrighteousness, against which one does well to cry out. Hence, to the vast majority of readers only jeremiads are acceptable. A paper which aimed at giving the Government side of questions would have no readers. Let it be remembered, also, that the Indian paper appeals to its public solely on the side of politics. In this strange literature there is no room for "City" intelligence, for literature, the drama, music, sport, fiction. The general news of the world is represented by a reprint of Reuter's telegrams of the day before clipped from a European journal; agriculture, the grand interest of the country, by a clipping from a Government bulletin, which, if the news happens to be bad, may furnish a

leaderette. But virtually the whole pith of
the-paper is in its politics, and its politics
consist in little more than a perpetual prejudicing of the acts and motives of the
Administration, spiced with attacks on the
personal iniquities of individual officers.

But what a Government, the European
reader may be inclined to think, to have
exposed itself to such a stream of invariable
criticism ! The answer is that it is precisely
the measures that the English reader would
most approve that have aroused much of the
most vehement opposition. A violent Hindu
agitation sprang up, for instance, against the
Bill brought forward and enacted by Lord
Lansdowne's Government for the protection
of child-wives married in form. Again, all
the agrarian legislation in which the Government has been periodically engaged for the
last forty years, which forms in the bulk an
achievement of enormous importance to the
masses on the land, has invariably been
opposed, whether in Bengal, the Punjab, the
United Provinces, or the Deccan, in a way
that might lead to the belief that the protection of the peasantry was the most unjust of
causes. Because a measure is of a " popular "
cast, therefore, this no more secures it a favour-

able reception than the heralding of Lord
Morley's constitutional reforms put a stop to
agitation. Even as far back as 1878, when
the Native Indian Press was a small affair,
comparatively speaking, Lord Lytton's
Government was obliged to take powers for
dealing with newspapers transgressing too
patently the liberty of free speech. The Act
could not be accused of working harshly, since
no prosecution was necessary under it; but
Lord Ripon repealed it, and since then the
story of the Indian Press has been-one of
successive accesses of violence, reluctantly
imposed checks, and fresh denunciations of
the restraint.

Once and again the Press has produced an
open-minded independent journalist like the
late Mr. Malabari of Bombay; and the rôle
should be a tempting one, for he who follows
it has the field to himself and is secure of the
appreciation of the rulers. Nevertheless, the
fact remains that these rare exceptions are
too few to count, and that the Press at large
is little more than an agency for creating
and organising an opinion unfavourable to
Government. It has already done a vast
deal of mischief, and it is, indeed, an open
question whether a free Press and a foreign

Administration, perpetually judged and mis-judged in face of a vast uncritical population, are institutions permanently compatible.

Since 1885 the forces of the Press have been backed up by the influence of the National Congress, whose attitude is also that of stand-ing opposition to the Government. The formation of this singular association was principally due to the late Mr. A. O. Hume, the ornithologist, who on retirement from the Civil Service seems to have been disposed to make things uncomfortable for the Govern-ment he had quitted. Mr. Hume started from certain positions to justify the move-ment he was setting on foot; one of which was the most extraordinary assertion ever enunci-ated by a man of his knowledge of the country. He said that in every village in India there were men who knew more and talked more of political affairs than could be found in any similar European societies. He maintained that vague stirrings of spirit were at work throughout the country, that the discontent-ment was becoming conscious of its possession of physical force, and that unless it were guided into constitutional channels of activity the end would be an explosion. The Congress, it may be observed, has been in activity for thirty years, and Mr. Hume's intelligent villagers are still absolutely indifferent to its existence. To do the originator justice, he foresaw this. The important part of his scheme was not the annual Parliamentary performance, but the formation of a corps of missionaries who should go out two by two, like the Apostles, and indoctrinate the villagers in their homes with a knowledge of their political rights and wrongs.

It does not require much acquaintance with India to judge what direction such a movement must have taken from the very start. But the gentlemen who assembled in the Congress pandal at Christmas had no fancy for spending the year in tramping the country as missionaries, and when Mr. Hume came to see that the National movement was to be confined to oratory and resolutions, his interest in it evaporated; and the other Englishmen who from time to time have taken a part in the Congress proceedings have been persons of quite a different type—publicists in search of a pedestal. Along with the occasional M.P., the Congress has now and again been able to put upon the dais a prominent Parsi or Mahomedan gentleman. The presence of these sympathisers served to justify the title "National," but did not alter the fact that the Congress has always been, until quite recently, a Hindu movement. The Mahomedans did not want it, and the Congress people did not want them, in any quantity.

Within the last year or two, however, the fresh exasperation of spirit produced by fresh reforms and promises of reforms to come has extended even to the Mahomedans, until at last their special organisation, the Moslem League, has formally joined causes with the Hindu Congress. Thus the Government is now confronted, for the first time, with the united opposition of the political classes in India. In another chapter an attempt will be made to show what this opposition seeks and what it signifies. Enough has been said above to indicate that the statement that the condition of the country is one of conspicuous loyalty requires considerable exceptions, which it will not do for the political reformer to put away as the work of an insignificant minority, seeing that this minority consists of the very classes with whom he is concerned, and to whom his "reward" is designed to appeal.

CHAPTER III

THE APPROACHING CLIMAX

THE shortest vision has been able to discern for some time past that things in India were working up inevitably to a crisis. The latter part of the Viceroyalty of Lord Hardinge, a diplomatist who, on coming to the business of conducting a Government on his own account, disclosed advanced political leanings, foreshadowed unmistakably what was coming, and the situation was brought to a head by the appointment of Mr. Montagu as Secretary of State, with the almost simultaneous announcement that Mr. Montagu was to transfer his office from Whitehall to Delhi to settle all difficulties out of hand by his presence on the spot. Reasons will be given in the sequel for opining that the mission he has undertaken with such alacrity raises the gravest cause for apprehension and the least prospect of any possible good result. Mr. Montagu acted under no compulsion; the invitation of the Viceroy to India was rather a confession of personal perplexity than a binding summons, and the war was the best of all reasons for retarding the consideration of fundamental changes. But Mr. Montagu as this is written has already reached the scene of his triumphs, the engagement is joined, and it will probably be left to Parliament and the British public to discuss the decisions arrived at after they have been announced in such a manner as to make subsequent discussion a business of form. Meantime, to appreciate the situation it is necessary to judge what the different parties are after. Mr. Montagu has explained his own position, and incidentally that of the Government, as far as in present times the Government is likely to have paid any attention to the matter, in his speech in the Commons in August announcing his forthcoming Indian tour. The passage is so important to the whole question that it must be quoted textually here. He said:

> The policy of His Majesty's Government, with which the Government of India are in complete accord, is that of the increasing association of Indians in every branch of the Administration, and the gradual development of self-governing institutions, with a view to the

progressive realisation of responsible government in India as an integral part of the British Empire. They have decided that substantial steps in this direction should be taken as soon as possible, and that it is of the highest importance as a preliminary to considering what these steps should be that there should be a free and informal exchange of opinion between those in authority at home and in India. His Majesty's Government have accordingly decided, with His Majesty's approval, that I should accept the Viceroy's invitation to proceed to India to discuss these matters with the Viceroy and the Government of India, to consider with the Viceroy the views of local governments, and to receive with him the suggestions of representative bodies and others. I would add that progress in this policy can only be achieved by successive stages. The British Government and the Government of India, on whom the responsibility lies for the welfare and advancement of the Indian peoples, must be the judges of the time and measure of each advance, and they must be guided by the co-operation received from those upon whom new opportunities of service will thus be conferred, and by the extent to which it is found that confidence can be reposed in their sense of responsibility. Ample opportunity will be afforded for public discussion of the proposals, which will be submitted in due course to Parliament.

This pronouncement gives us, at any rate, what Mr. Montagu means. It indicates the pressing home of a policy on the recognised lines of British Radicalism. The next thing is to see what the Indian political opposition means; what other Indian interests mean; what that ignored factor, the European element, means; finally, what changes in the direction of " the development of self-governing institutions with a view to the realisation of responsible government " are likely to mean. In regard to the Indian political body there is no difficulty in ascertaining its aims, or, as the phrase goes now, its aspirations, for these people, with their natural instinct for the tactics of agitation, admit no differences to appear as to the articles of their programme. The Congress practice of passing year after year a number of identical resolutions, many of which were, at any rate when the meetings started, totally outside the regions of practical possibility, had the effect of giving these demands, by dint of constant iteration, the appearance of unredressed grievances with a great volume of opinion behind them. The note of a particular session might vary according to the temperament, responsibility, experience, of the President and managers of that

year's gathering, but the items of the omnibus
resolution, such as repeal of the Arms Act,
the complete separation of executive and
judicial powers, have been acquiring solidity
by age and repetition. At a time when
provincial decentralisation and provincial
independence have come under increasing
discussion as the lines along which Indian
administration should develop in the future,
there is no sign whatever of difference of provincial sentiments or interests being at work
in the Congress or, indeed, among the Indian
members of the Viceroy's Council. On the
contrary, the clue of the politicals is always
to suppress from view all notice of local
distinctions and divergences, to speak of
India as one, demanding the same measures
and the same remedies with equal urgency by
the mouth of one public opinion. Whether
this leaning to unity may be ultimately trace-
able, as the political philosopher might maintain, to the physical character of the country,
or whether it is an effect of the uniformity of
ideas produced by a State system of education, or whether it comes naturally to a
people with a highly developed aptitude for
getting round their rulers, this convention
of a single political interest and opinion

is the most characteristic feature of the
agitation.

It was exhibited with delightful uncon-
sciousness by His Highness the Aga Khan in
a letter to *The Times* last autumn, which
deplored that there was no Member from
India sitting in Parliament, like the late Mr.
Dadabhai Naoroji, who could have given the
House the Indian view ! As though there
could be no shade of difference in the view
that every man in Hindustan must take of
such a subject as the Montagu - Chelmsford
projects ! Singleness of opinion carried to
this extent can only mean that there is no
real public opinion—and this is rather the
trouble in India.

As it is, it does not require an Indian M.P.,
in the shape of a Parsi gentleman domiciled
in London, to discover for us *the* Indian view
of the Aga Khan. Although the front of the
Congress line is allowed to present no appearance of diversity, it is not in itself stationary.
It is, in fact, always advancing. The reforms
outlined in the political testament of Mr.
Gokhale, published to the world last May, are
already pronounced to be behind time and
obsolete. The school of Mr. Gokhale, the

party of Moderates, which Lord Morley elaborately played to capture and bring over, is already out of the running. "We really pity those members of the European community," an Indian paper recently declared, "who try to delude themselves or others that there is such a party as Moderates in this country." Why be a Moderate and put up with petty concessions when Home Rule is dangling within reach? Why, indeed? And the upshot is that the midway men and the gradual progress men have to come up into the front line. What the political Indian wishes, as most of us would wish if we were in his place, is to see the last of the British altogether. The difference (the unfortunate difference if the reader likes) is that the Indians who would see us gone are perfectly incapable of filling the vacancy for themselves. The captains of the movement are well aware of this, and therefore do not at all recommend the severance of the connection. "Home Rule within the Empire" is a good substitute, promising all the pleasantness to India and all the gravamen to the Empire. The white ensign would still protect, for a trifle of £100,000 per annum, the argosies from the Thames and Mersey, which would yield up

just as much of their value in the way of
duties as would not prevent the trade from
dying out altogether. A British Army would
be obviously indispensable, not only for the
sake of protection against external intruders,
but because the Indian Army, if left by itself,
or some one of its component elements, Sikh,
Mussalman, or Gurkha, might assume a
disagreeable predominance. The maintenance of the Viceroyalty on the status of that
of Canada would be desirable as giving dignity
and stability to the new Government, and as
providing a check against inconvenient pretensions on the part of any of the Native
Princes.

Thus safeguarded and guaranteed, the
Indian politician looks forward jubilantly to
the establishment of a national Government
invested with the full power of the purse, with
the making of the laws in Councils, Central
and Provincial, in which his party is to have
a complete preponderance, with the complete
control of the Executive, and of the administration of justice. To ensure a free hand to
the new dispensation, the functions of the
Secretary of State for India are to be reduced
to those of the Colonial Secretary *quâ* his
relations with the self-governing Dominions,

and the India Council abolished.   Given this starting-point, the reformers wisely do not insist on the immediate and complete disappearance of the British element from the Councils, the public services, or from trade and business within the country.   Men with much less gift for political manipulation could see that with self-government conceded, the rest would follow of itself.   The European, official or non-official, would remain simply on toleration, since the new Government could at any time make his position unendurable.   The abandonment of authority as the principle of Government in favour of that of popular volition too obviously means the surrender of the whole British position in India, and complete capitulation to the agitators even before they had in their own minds begun to think seriously of success.

It is true that the sympathetic entertainers who roll up the edge of the curtain to disclose to the gratified audience entrancing visions of the times to come—Lord Hardinge, Lord Chelmsford, Mr. Montagu—at the same time warn them that the realisation must take a long time, some indefinite time, and adjure them to tranquillity and patience.   It is no wonder that the tail of the discourse is the least heeded portion. If the things promised them are so good and so wholesome, why should there be all this delay in their bestowal? Why should they even be deferred in deference to the continuation of the war, which does not touch Indian domestic politics ? The agitators, in fact, recognise that the distraction of the British public in the war is their great opportunity, and therefore the Montagu-Chelmsford pronouncements were a signal to them, and one cannot blame them therein, for raising the pitch of the reform cry. With infantile simplicity, the Indian public of all sections was exhorted to co-operate in preserving a "calm," an artificial calm, during the visit of Mr. Montagu, in order that the two intellects that had undertaken the settlement of these high concerns might work undisturbed; as though it were probable, or indeed, on the democratic theory, desirable, that great masses of people with the most divergent interests should look on in religious silence while their destinies were being settled for them, or content themselves with a memorandum in statement of case. The inevitable result of the Montagu proceedings was an immediate spread of agitation, in which classes hitherto regarded as inaudible have been stimulated to combine and remonstrate lest their interests should be disposed of unnoticed.

The seed of the climax to which we are now approaching was sown in a far-back day when someone invented the phrase "India for the Indians." The saying summarises in four words a whole train of argument which there is no shame in admitting has a peculiar cogency for the British conscience; and if the Indians were a homogeneous people, if they were capable of defending their own country on our withdrawal, of forming a Government that could be trusted to discharge the obligations which would be incurred on the transfer, if they were even reasonably unanimous in desiring us to be gone, Britannia, however painful the consideration, might feel herself forced to consider whether she was not under moral obligation to wind up her Hindustan branch of ·business. She would be back on that other saying, a still older one, that the only Indian question is how to get well away from India. But the smallest reflection will show that none of the conditions exist that would allow the matter to be brought to this simple issue.

In the actual circumstances all that the phrase "India for the Indians" does for us is to suggest the question, Which Indians? As things stand, there is first the great cleavage of the population into the opposing bodies of Hindus and Mahomedans, whose historical antagonism is fully maintained in the minds of the masses to-day. Next, within the Hindu fold there are racial divisions —for example, Rajputs, Bengalis, Beharis, Mahrattas, Dravidians, Jats, etc., people who have little in common but the acknowledgment of Brahmanism and the worship of the cow. Nearer to the Rajput and the Jat physically come the Sikhs, who are not Hindus. Further, between Hindus of the same country there are all the divisions of caste, separating them into watertight compartments socially; and yet again there are castes which are divided internally by being part Hindu and part Mahomedan. Then there are people who may have some tincture of Hinduism, but are ethnically totally different from all these, such as the Nepalese and the population of the Himalayan region. Add to these people who are separate from any of the above and from each other in race, religion, and character, the Burmans; the aboriginal tribes of Central India and the Central Provinces; those of Orissa and the adjoining States; the tribes of Assam hills and frontier tracts; the peoples of the Divide between Burma and Assam and between Burma and Chittagong. This congeries includes people in every state and degree of civilisation, from the Jain mystic who fears to take the life of a flea to the Lushai who till the other day was a professional head-hunter. It includes also nearly 4,000,000 Native Christians, mostly in a very depressed social condition.

The single common tie running through this variegated conglomeration of humanity is allegiance to the British Power, and their consciousness of the fact was touchingly manifested at the King's Durbar in 1911, which gave the sentiment an opportunity of expression. That great demonstration showed that the central fact of an all-powerful, just, benevolent Government had come to appeal to minds which would scarcely have been supposed receptive to any political ideas. Yet, after all, it is not astonishing that a foreign Government should not be debarred from the attachment of people to whom a Bengali, for instance, is equally a foreigner. It is not to be imagined that the great majority

of the outer circles have any notion of what
is preparing for them between Whitehall and
Delhi; but the knowledge of the impending
changes afoot seems to have spread further
down and more rapidly than would have been
expected, and it immediately provoked apprehension and remonstrance to an extent truly
significant considering the unenlightened, un-
organised communities from which the
counter-demonstrations spring. The beginning came from Madras, a Province which
probably contains a greater mixture of races
and conditions than any other, the Brahman
influence being securely established at the top
of the pyramid. Here Mr. Montagu's boon
of representation is interpreted as boding
the absolute ascendancy of the Brahman,
and it is with this fear that the protest
meetings have been continually occupied.
But even in Calcutta, the particular preserve
of the Babu and the agitator, home of a people
whose mind is stayed on the repetition of
political commonplaces—even there we are
met with symptoms of reaction, public meetings of the lower castes who have taken the
alarm in earnest now that they see that there
is a real danger of reforms which will mean
for them subjection.

Above all, the knowledge that an extension of representative institutions is impending has been sufficient to arouse the latent antagonism between Mahomedan and Hindu in a way that discloses the thinness of the film of agreement by which the Congress and Moslem League leaders professed to have closed over the gulf.   Within a few weeks of Mr. Montagu's announcement the most formidable Hindu-Mahomedan riot of recent times had broken out in the tranquil province of Behar.   At the time of writing there is no information available beyond the accounts in newspapers of the evidence given at the trial of some of the rioters, but there seems to have been a prearranged movement throughout the Hindu countryside to pick a quarrel with the Mahomedans over the sacrificial festival called Bakr'idd, and to "let them have it."   The purpose was thoroughly effected; the Mussalmans, being in a great minority, were helpless, and the police could not cope with the mobs of villagers.   In over one hundred villages their houses were broken open and sacked, and the occupants, men and women, plundered and maltreated.   In a district where formerly not a company of sepoys had been necessary, order had to be restored last October by patrols of British Cavalry and Horse Artillery.

In itself this Arrah disturbance has clearly no " political " significance whatever. It was an eruption of a hostility which is always ready to break out, opportunity offering; but a combination among villagers on such scale —some of the mobs are said to have numbered thousands—points to the existence of a general belief that the hold of British authority is relaxing.* Probably this belief has been

* This view of the case is confirmed by the reports of the trials still arriving from India. Thus in one case, known as the Bazidpur riot, which came before the Gaya Tribunal, Counsel for the Crown in his opening said: "This riot was led by the Babu of Narga, otherwise known as Sheonandan Singh. This young man, as the evidence would show, was a man of considerable *zemindari* and very highly connected. He was on horseback leading the mob. He was made to believe by some Hindu pandits that he was destined to be the Raja of the Province of Behar, and with this he started on the work of leading the rioters. This idea originated under a misconception that the Government was weakening, and that this was a most opportune time to terrorise the Mahomedans." To illustrate the seriousness of the riots a quotation may be added from the judgment of the Court in the Mauna case, one of those which came before the Arrah Tribunal.

The Commissioners, in their judgment, say: "The

implanted in the rural mind by the tall talk of agitators; partly, too, it may have arisen from vague impressions of the success of the political agitation itself as measured by the rumours of concessions, which the country-side would attribute to anything rather than such an incomprehensible cause as the democratic sentiment. But whenever the peasantry get to think that they have a free hand, they will set about working off their own grievances in their own way—debtor

---

attack on Mauna is a grim and moving story. The isolated position of this Mahomedan village, the distribution of *patias* inciting to its loot, the determination of the Mahomedans to resist, the erection of barricades, the five hours' battle, in the course of which the thousands of Hindus were more than once repulsed by the defenders, the subsequent murders, rape, arson, sacrilege, and loot—it was difficult to imagine that scenes like this had recently taken place in the peaceful district of Shahabad without the slightest justification or provocation. Mauna is a village inhabited almost entirely by Mahomedans, some of whom are the maliks of the village and are men of position. Many of the witnesses were of a different class from those in the previous cases which had come before us. They were obviously, both from their physique and bearing, Mahomedans of a superior class. It was, no doubt, due to this circumstance—namely, that they had among them real leaders —that such a well-designed and desperate defence was made."

against moneylender, tenant against landholder, Mahomedan against Hindu, or *vice
versa*. So they did in the Mutiny, and so
they will act again if they get the chance; and
the lesson of the Behar riots is that after a
few years of a Delhi Parliament, supported
by indigenous official agency, the country
people might be found to have become a very
different set of beings from the *rayats* of the
present day, whose docility we are apt to
take for granted. In fact, it may be said in
all seriousness that if the British could with-
draw absolutely from India, having secured
from the League of Nations an understanding
that no other Power should attempt to take
its place, the earliest result would be that the
new Government would find itself faced with
a turbulent population quite beyond its
capacities of management. This consideration is not one to occur to the democratic
reformer, but it is one that should be duly
pondered by John Bull before he signs the
deed of transfer.

For the moment, however, the Behar commotion, followed by a disturbance which
occurred soon after at Allahabad on the
occasion of the Mohurram procession, which

was only kept under by elaborate and timely precautions, has had a direct bearing on the political situation. The Mahomedan community, outraged in its sentiments and alarmed, has very generally repudiated the All-India Moslem League—which, in spite of its big name, has a small basis—and its compact with the Congress, and Mahomedan gatherings are being reported at the time of writing from all over India to insist on the separate standing of their community, and the necessity of supranumerical provisions and guarantees in order that it may be assured of justice. Add to this the memorials with which Mr. Montagu is being plied by sectional interests, from the Talukdars (Barons) of Oudh . downwards, demanding that their several parties must receive very special consideration in any fair scheme of representation, and it will be seen that his *Veni, vidi, vici,* is not such a simple affair.

CHAPTER IV

THE PROPOSED REMEDY

THE situation as it now presents itself may well be judged as an extraordinary one. A scheme of reforms evidently of the most far-reaching and incalculable effect is being thrust upon the public with every suggestion of some extreme urgency. In any ordinary circumstances the existence of the war would have been sufficient reason for postponing the introduction of measures of this character till a season more suitable for deliberation; but these, it appears, must come before the smoke of the cannon has blown away. The reason can only be that those in authority suppose that the discontent in India is too serious to allow of an instant's delay in the application of the remedy; and when the remedy is looked at it is only another brew of the very drugs that have produced the present unlikeable symptoms—the same prescription, but a stronger dose. What an admission of inefficacy in the past, what a dismal omen for

future persistence in the same line of endeavour! This need for tranquillising concessions with which Lord Chelmsford and Mr.
Montagu are so urgently impressed, does it
arise out of popular indignation at the short-
comings of the Government or a popular
yearning after another kind of government ?
There is no sort of doubt that no need lies
here. The Government of India has its
defects, of course, but it has been hitherto a
very excellent Government, full of the spirit
of improvement, high-motived, just and effi-
cient, at any rate to a degree which is far
beyond the critical faculties of its subjects.
The Legislative Councillor of the Viceroy's
Council finds practically no fault with what it
does; the unending stream of disapproval and
vituperation in the Press contains a minimum
of suggestions for improvement. In candid
moments it is admitted that the only fault of
the Government is that it is not a Government of the people; but as a Government of
the people of India does not stand analysis,
the favourite reproach against the existing
system is that of being a bureaucracy. This
villainous compound has been adopted by the
Indian [publicist as an advanced term of
reproach, and when he calls the Government

by that name and upbraids its members
as bureaucrats, it is with the air of one who
has left the accused without answer or extenu-
ation.   But at the same time, if we follow the
speaker and his school into particulars, we
shall find that his most prominent demands
are for larger Executive Councils with more
Indian members; he calls for more Indian
secretaries, more Indian magistrates, more
Indian Civilians in all capacities, and more
Indians in every department of the Administration, until in the golden age, more or less
approximate according to the colour of his
politics, the whole corps of public servants
will consist of Indians entirely.   It is a very
natural ambition, but it does not betray
any objection to bureaucracy.   In point of
fact, no objection to the system which he
denounces has ever occurred to him.   If he
were mentally the heir of the English school
whose language he borrows he would necessarily recognise the inconsistency of his
position.   Logically, it must be one thing or
the other: either a reformer wants the extension of representative government, which
supersedes bureaucracy, or he wants good
bureaucracy, which supersedes representative government,

No one knowing the country can have the faintest doubt on which side the prepossessions of the critics lie. It is perfectly impossible that men with the heredity of the Indians should suddenly become convinced adherents of principles of government which are foreign to all their traditions and experience. It is possible that a community of Africans, say like the people of Liberia, subjected to Western influence, might develop a sudden enthusiasm for the ideas of political equality and democracy, as on occasions they become wholesale converts to Mahomedanism or Christianity, but it is not possible that Hindus should undergo these violent transformations. The Brahman cannot look forward with satisfaction to the prospect of a governing proletariat. As long as they lived to themselves, the Hindus lived under a system in which moral, political, and social affairs were regulated by a code which professed to stand on Divine authority. Political and social doings being closely bound up with religious observances, the whole structure became immutable. Their institutions included monarchy as the inevitable form of government, and to this day, when a writer is moved to rhapsodise over the King-Emperor,

he often falls back on the Hindu idea that the
royal authority is an emanation of the Divine
power.   Not only did the Hindus never think
of any other form of government but the
kingship, but the Mahomedans, when they
came into possession, were equally monarchi-
cal in practice.   The influence that Hindu
sentiment gradually worked upon their minds
is clearly shown in the immense outward
reverence paid to the last to the authority of
the Moghul Emperor long after he had ceased
to have any; so that a Subahdar (Satrap) or
Nawab, even when in rebellion, would attach
the highest importance to getting a decree
out of Delhi to sanction the very acquisitions
to which he was helping himself at the
expense of the central power.

In all the countless changes of dynasty,
risings and fallings of races and powers, of
which Indian history contains the record,
there seems to be no instance of the Indian
mind having hit upon any other type of
government but the sovereignty of a single
ruler.   Is it to be supposed, then, that a
people with such a past can in the course of
two or three decades have become genuinely
converted to a political faith which runs
counter to all the ideas they have so stead-

fastly manifested ?   One may perhaps be
told that in the great State of Mysore the
Maharaja's Government has of its own accord
set up an assembly of the people, which meets
once a year and ratifies an account of State
affairs presented to it by the Minister; and
an interesting experiment this Assembly is,
and perhaps might have been more heeded
by our own Government. But in Mysore,
by all accounts, the real power is entirely in
the hands of an oligarchy of very able Brahman officials, and it is just because they are
united and their ascendancy is unquestioned
that the Government is successful, and they
can afford to make picturesque concessions to
the popular element.   The extenson of representative institutions in India would bear no
resemblance to the Councils and Assemblies
of Mysore, Bikanir, and one or two other
progressive States where no one dreams of
disputing the ultimate authority of the Chief.

Representative institutions, says Lord
Acton in one of his essays, presuppose the
unity of a people. The history of British
politics since Ireland was taken over to
Westminster is enough to suggest how much
truth there is in the dictum. But the House

of Commons, with the Irish element included, is a model of homogeneity and simplicity to the conditions that representation will have to adapt itself to in India. The working of the system in almost any case means the setting aside of the rights and interests of important minorities; but here the sections left out in the cold would be majorities, huge majorities, but lacking the intelligence, education, social standing, and so forth, to give them any part in the scheme. We shall also come to see that it not only puts on one side the peasantry, the Indian Christian, the depressed classes, the aboriginal millions, but that it also leaves out of account that minority to which the present position of the country before the world is wholly due—namely, the European element, in the services and non-official.

Finally, the idea of regenerating India by virtue of representative institutions overlooks the existence of a very large class which plays a part of immense importance in the social life of the country, but which, because it holds aloof from the Press and platform, is ignored entirely by political reformers.

I will suppose that we are approaching across country a small market town anywhere in Upper India. At the outskirts, just as we are expecting to enter it and to gain our tents in the camping grove beyond, we have to make a detour of a quarter of a mile, for the reason that where the road crosses a small ravine by a bridge a tree has fallen, obstructing the route. To clear away the obstacle would have taken eight or ten men a couple of hours' work; and so the carts have discovered a way round to a point where the gully is just passable for wheeled traffic. We follow the now well-worn track and arrive in the main street. The place is very much as a village grown large except that one sees a few brick houses of some pretensions among the huts of the bazaar, a post office, and a police station. The grain and vegetable shops, too, of the village are reinforced by a good sprinkling of confectioners, their sweets shadowed by clouds of wasps and hornets, which, however, never seem to be aggressive, and alongside the sweetmeat stalls are others which display British scissors and knives, looking-glasses, and possibly the ubiquitous sewing-machine. At the back of the establishment will probably be hanging a highly coloured portrait of His Majesty the King, and perhaps on the whitewashed wall

outside a chalk representation of a British
Tommy, also in full uniform, in difficulties
with a tiger. One must not grudge the Hindu
his joke, which he takes so rarely. Farther on
we may come upon specimens of the local
industry—if there is one—pottery, metal
work or embroidery, as the case may be.
Then, if the place is at all flourishing, the
best sites will be taken up by two or three
houses of a superior size and style, in which
neatness and propriety are conspicuous.
There is the grain merchant, whose ground
floor is lined with rows of sacks, suggesting
business on the commercial scale; there is the
sonar (goldsmith), who is jeweller, banker,
and money-changer in one; there is also the
cloth-merchant surrounded by a goodly stock
of bales. Here the owners, in contrast with
the noisy retailers of the lower bazaar, are
silent, unemotional persons, of composed
manners, always ready for business, but never
forcing it on the passer-by. In each shop
will be noticed in the different corners two
or three small boys, the sons of the house,
taking stock with præternatural gravity of
all that is going on. When old enough these
born merchants will go to the local school to
imbibe as much as will be useful to them for

G

their purposes in life. In the afternoon they
return to their places of observation in the
shop, watching with their large round eyes the
transactions that pass, and in the intervals
studying the special script that is a secret of
the profession. After fifteen or eighteen
years of a life of such concentration the boy,
who has never known boyhood, is a trader
equipped at all points. Let us suppose him
to have been launched into the world on a
larger scale in the charge of some relative
in a bigger way of business. We may meet
him next in one of the centres of country
trade, where the merchants are working on
the large scale in cotton, wheat, oil seeds, or
whatever is the local speciality of the market.
We find him in the company of men like himself, his reserve by this time somewhat
thawed by contact with the world, alert, intelligent men of simple habits, whose affluence
is only allowed to appear in a pearl ear-ring,
who are doing large deals in produce or imports, coupled often with simple speculations
in silver or Government paper. They are a
friendly circle, and one of them readily under-
takes to show you round to the head banker
of the Province, who will provide you with
hundis, the equivalent of a circular letter

of credit, on his different correspondents
in the towns you are likely to be visiting
during a forthcoming tour in the interior.
We call at the great man's house in the heart
of the town, approached down a narrow lane,
much crowded with cows and beggars, expecting alike the daily dole. A small low door,
flanked by a still smaller barred window,
gives access to a narrow passage which opens
on to a bare apartment furnished with a chair
or two and the custodian's quilt done into a
roll in one corner. A heavy curtain shuts off
the interior of the house. The banker probably has a garden house or two in pleasant
spots outside the town where he spends the
afternoon occasionally, to enjoy the breeze;
but it is to this cave that he returns on the
hottest nights so as to sleep among his books,
and to be at work early. Presently the
millionaire enters, a good-looking man, dressed
in plain white with a fine Kashmir shawl over
his shoulders. The business is soon done,
and as you take your leave he lets you know
that a motor-car or a carriage is at your dis-
posal during your stay in the place. The
English residents soon get to know him better,
for he is probably the owner of two-thirds of
the residential bungalows in the Station, and

looks after his house property vigilantly. If Major Jones has to complain that his thatch is letting in the rain, it is the Lala Sahib himself who will come round to verify the mischief, to see that his agent does not charge him a rupee too much for the repairs. A hard man of business and a remorseless creditor, in spite of his care for the pence he can be liberal on occasion, entertaining European society in honour of nuptials between boys and girls whom they do not know at banquets which he does not share; and often giving largely to public objects, besides building the inevitable river-side temple and bathing-place to preserve his name amongst his fellow-townsmen. He is in many respects the most powerful man in the district, perhaps in a whole group of districts, but he shows no inclination to move beyond his own line, least of all to carry his influence into politics. Of what good are discontent and agitation to people whose interests are bound up with social security ? Sett, Mahajan, Marwari, Chetty, Bora, Buniya, Shroff, as they are known in different parts, or according to diversities of business, there is no class in India that is so homogeneous in tastes, habits, and aptitudes, as these men of finance, and

the only side of our public life that at all
appeals to them is municipal politics.   Here
real, tangible interests are affected in the provisions of the ways and means for meeting
local expenditure, octroi versus house tax,
the incidence of a water rate, building regulations, and so on, to say nothing of the important province of municipal contracts.   Thus
the business class in self-defence have to see
to it that local affairs are not left wholly in
the hands of the lawyers; but in politics in
the ordinary sense they, until recent times
the only middle class in the country, refuse to
be interested.   Even a collected community
like the Marwaris, the Indian " City " of Calcutta, show no leanings towards politics in
the Bengali sense, and the men of the business castes up-country are too few and too
scattered to be able to make themselves felt
if the will were there.   So they stand aside
and put their faith in the equal justice of a
benevolent Government, which seems likely
as it comes over to modern ways to treat
them with the disregard that is the general
reward of all who cannot or will not make
themselves unpleasant.*

* It may be objected that this sketch is a misrepre-
sentation of business society as it exists, for instance,

It would seem, therefore, that the most cursory glance over the conditions is sufficient to suggest that the new policy can only come out at a parody of self-government, accompanied by dire injustice and ill-consequences to the interests ignored. But it may be said at this point that there are already representative institutions in existence in the shape of the Legislative Councils, imperial and provincial, which have surely worked well enough hitherto, and, to judge by the compliments which are continually being paid to them, must be filling a useful place in the public economy. To extend the powers of bodies which have already found their place in the world cannot surely be anything more than an innocuous advance on lines already tried. The answer is that the Legislative Councils, expanded as they have been, are in no sense Parliaments. The tracing of their development in detail by its successive steps would be a long matter, but they are all

---

in the great centre of Bombay. The answer is that the business world of Bombay, with its mixture of elements, is like nothing else in India, just as the Bombay Municipal Corporation, with its own lively politics and its seats the object of social ambition, is a thing *sui generis*.

of precisely the same type, after the manner
of Indo-British institutions which have been
developed with little regard to provincial
variety. If a province was socially backward
it went without a Legislative Council, but
when it was judged to have advanced sufficiently it was served out with one of the
standard pattern. This, again, was derived
from the constitution of the original of the
class, the Legislative Council of India.

Until 1833 the making of the laws had
rested, along with the other functions of
government, in the hands of the Governor-
General's Executive Council. In that year a
special member was added to this Cabinet
to take charge of legislative work, who was
to be an English lawyer, and the first choice
fell upon the future Lord Macaulay. The
business of law-making naturally grew more
complicated, and in 1853 the Legislative
Council was formally recognised. The
members of the Executive Council were now
reinforced by a few high officials from different
provinces concerned in pending legislation,
generally by the Chief Justice of Bengal, by
a member from the Calcutta business community, and three or four Indians of dis-
tinction. But the Council was practically a

Committee of Government for the purposes
of legislation, and its offshoots have preserved
the character of the institution from which
they have grown. The executive element
remains the nucleus.

In each Provincial Council the Governor or
Lieutenant-Governor presides, the members
of the Executive Council or the Secretaries to
Government, as the case may be, are the Front
Bench, but there is no Opposition. The
remainder of the Chamber, whether officials
or non-officials, are merely additional members,
and as there is no question of upsetting the
Government, it might have been said until
recently that the common object was to give
the country the best laws. When there was
no legislative business on hand a Council did
not meet. From 1861 to 1892 this was the
position. A year or two before the latter date
the Government of India had come to the conclusion that an extension of the system was
required, both as a concession to Indian
political sentiment and for furnishing the
Government with a means of expounding its
views and measures to the community. In
the reform that resulted the Councils were
enlarged in size; the right of returning a
member or members was conferred on certain

outside bodies of recognised status, such as the Universities, clusters of Municipal Corporations and of District Boards, and the Chambers of Commerce; and internally the boundaries of business were enlarged by the discussion of the several Budgets irrespectively of their involving legislation and the extension of the right of questioning.

As an opiate for the political classes, the administration of which was not then the all-powerful consideration it has since become, the change was no success, and in the following decade came the further developments of Lord Morley, of which the same must be said. Under Lord Morley's scheme the numbers of the elected members increased, but those of the nominated members were increased *pari passu,* so as to hold them in check. This, and such changes as that resolutions could be introduced on subjects unconnected with legislative proposals, and that the Budgets should be considered in advance by a Committee including certain non-official members, could not appeal to the opposition outside. In the case of the Viceroy's Council there was a short period during which it seemed that under the personal influence of Mr. Gokhale a critical opposition might be built up within the Council itself, which, expressing the wants and wishes of the educated party throughout the country in the best way, might take the wind out of the sails of the agitators pure and simple; but the development he seemed to be working for rested on his own ascendancy, and disappeared with him.

It is impossible for the rest that the Legislative Councils on their present basis should satisfy the outside political agitation. Though they are to an extent representative, the representation is of certain interests arbitrarily selected and fixed by Government; their numbers are small, varying from sixty-eight in the case of the Viceroy's Council to eighteen in the case of the Legislative Council of Burma; their proceedings are restricted to defined subjects; and the word of the Government is the ultimate law even down to the results of a division. It would, of course, be possible to introduce a direct franchise, to treble or quadruple the number of seats, as the agitators demand, with the result of swamping the official and nominated members and sweeping away Government control, but they would then have become something totally different from what they are or were ever intended to be. From being a branch of the Government they would be installed in the mastery, and there would be no object in retaining for them a delusive title.

But although the preceding attempts to reform these Councils while preserving their character has had no effect in mitigating the tone of the outside opposition, it would be a mistake to suppose that their enlargement has not been popular with the classes who come personally into the circle of their influence. The Indians are born Parliament men, who love to have their talk out in public on all joint affairs, from the conference in which each caste arranges its own concerns onwards. A large proportion of them are ready speakers and almost all are good listeners. No one can read the proceedings of any Indian Council without being struck by the number of subjects that are brought forward by means of resolutions merely for the sake of ventilation; also, he will soon notice that many of these are old public favourites which have had many an airing before, but that this does not at all deter each Indian member, as his turn comes, from furnishing his contribution to the subject, identical though it may be with the opinions expressed by half a dozen honourable colleagues before him. The British-made rules of procedure must be a constant trial to these members, but they are accepted with exemplary patience and decorum; and, on the other hand, though the verbosity of many Indian members and their quenchless thirst for information, as manifested in the question paper, is a trial to such busy men as Members of Council and Secretaries, there is no doubt that the association of the Legislative Council does a great deal in the way of promoting personal understanding.

It is not probable that in regard to the opinion of this or that section of the public the Indian element tells the Government anything that it would not otherwise know. It is not the way of the class to lay bare their minds. They speak the sentiments they feel to be expected of their station and circumstances, and if an Indian Councillor had any serious message for the head of the province he would ask for an interview and would give it privately. But the social intercourse that is brought about in the course of business is all to the good, and only on this account few responsible officials would go back on the present system if they could,

They know that they like the Indian Councillor the better for seeing more of him, and he in turn is usually responsive to the friendliness he is met with. The misfortune is that the Indian Councillor, however broadened by the experience of his office, counts for so little outside. He is usually a person who has already " arrived ": a landowner, put forward by his class for his knowledge of English, or a successful lawyer, or someone who has made a name by municipal work. Such men as these do not want to remould the scheme of things, but the opposition outside does. This uneasy multitude, whose menacing proportions stimulate the progress of our British reformers, is not interested in measures of which they could approve. The result is that the Legislative Councillors are of no avail at all as a breakwater to the Government which has created them. They can swell an agitation with much effect, if they are so minded, but they are powerless to lay one. So that the Government in England, if it concludes to endorse Mr. Montagu's undertaking to regenerate India by means of representative institutions, will be left to choose whether it will take refuge in concessions so safeguarded that discontent and sedition will be as active as before, or it will throw open the way to advances which must surely and speedily render the British position in the country untenable. For to confer independent powers on an Indian Parliament and to think to check the results afterwards, when any interference with "the popular will" would be trebly resented, is clearly chimerical. But whatever other tendencies an Indian Parliament might manifest, its action would assuredly not take the line of lessening the numbers or the influence of the bureaucracy.

CHAPTER V

THE REAL OPPOSITION

THE people who have been brought into direct contact with the Administration, like the Legislative Councillors of the last chapter and the numerous body of officials in the public services, if they are not opposed to the agitators in sympathy, are in the main a well-disposed, tractable class, conscious of the power of Government and keenly alive to the value of the decorations and titles in its gift.* Unfortunately, it may be repeated, these classes have no active influence; and we come next to those outside the gate, the general body of the educated, and more particularly the English educated, whose attitude is beyond question. This English educated phalanx may be said to number about a million and a half of persons, which, on strict democratic principles, would not entitle it to

* The Birthday and New Year *Gazettes* are awaited in India by those concerned with an expectancy surpassing even that of democratic England.

a commanding voice in the destinies of a
population of three hundred millions, but it
is the only voice which the British public
hears. It includes all the lawyers, all the
influential journalists, and all the students of
the high schools and colleges. And the serious
feature of the situation is that it is just the
present generation of students, the men of
to-morrow, who are most embittered. It
would be absurd to pronounce a sweeping
opinion on a subject of such extent, as
the tone in different provinces varies, and,
of course, one college may differ from another
in iniquity; but as far as may be gathered
from those, such as educational officers, who
have had exceptional opportunities of forming
a judgment, the sentiments of this young India
are practically solid against us. In a sense it is
only natural that young men should develop
violent opinions. Our own undergraduates
often enough flutter off into Socialism, and
even Tom Brown became a Republican, for a
few months, during his stay at Oxford. But
the Indian has not the same chance of shed-
ding his extravagances later on by rubbing
shoulders with men of different upbringing
and experience. A universal State system
of education turns out men of a similar

pattern, and all the result of the British State system of education in India is that it is producing a type increasingly antagonistic to the authority which introduced it and presides over its working.

After all, the dismal result is not really so paradoxical as it would seem. The Englishman of the school which has generally had the last word in affairs during the past century is a person who is totally indifferent to the element of national psychology. He would deal out his own law and his own political theory to distant Asiatics regardless even of the modifications he might borrow from the practice of Continental neighbours in dealing with their own subjects, with an unquestioning confidence that the results will be in accordance with his own intentions. Yet there is nothing more certain than that the same institutions become different things when applied by men whose ideas and antecedents are different. On the subject of the differences between the European peoples and the Indian peoples a volume might be written by a competent pen. They are always making themselves felt in practice to the legislator and administrator, and the

7

manner of it is this: Some new experiment is
introduced, and for a time gives great promises
of fulfilment in the European sense; then it
goes astray on a different line of its own, an
Oriental line.   The reason is that as long as
the experiment was under the direction and
control of a few select minds its tone and
character conformed to their intentions.   But
as the new departure succeeds it loses its
identity and takes its colour and form from
those upon whom it has been introduced.
One instance is the Indian Press, which,
instead of spreading information and enter-
tainment, has become a mere gramophone of
grievances.   It is interesting to speculate on
what form Indian Christianity would have
by now taken, had the country undergone
the wholesale conversion which the missionaries of an earlier day expected as soon as
education and printing should have spread
abroad.   Indian Christianity would by this
time have certainly become something very
different from British evangelical Christianity;
but in the result the Hindu held fast to his
own religion, while he accepted with avidity
the education offered him, and is gradually
transforming it according to his own ideas
and circumstances.

A system of which the plan was devised
by the most robust of Westerners, Lord
Macaulay, and which was introduced in the
first instance with the practical aim of providing a class of officials to meet the wants of
an expanding Administration, has found a soil
in which it has thrown out roots of its own
from which a prodigious growth is springing.
The officials of the Department of Public
Instruction who nominally retain control are
constantly engaged in endeavouring to trim
its luxuriance, but it has got beyond them.
Indian education is a social phenomenon
which is being shaped by forces within. In
the schools the Department, with its grants
and inspections, can still keep nominally the
direction of affairs and insist on conformity to
the code, but the colleges and Universities are
emancipating themselves and taking their own
line of development. Consciously or subcon-
sciously, Government interference is resented.
Nothing in Lord Curzon's full programme of
measures cost him such genuine loss of popu-
larity as his stirring the question of University
reform. It was difficult at the time to account
for the bitterness of the opposition to an
essentially reasonable measure, but since then
the contest has been renewed on each occa-

sion of the foundation of a new University. The Government strives to retain a measure of control by reserving the right of nomination to the chief offices and the governing body and in the distribution of powers. By the opposition every reservation is resisted to the utmost, until the matter closes with the inevitable compromise. There is nothing on which the Indian mind is so much set as a great extension of Universities. I forget how many Mr. Gokhale once gave as the number which he eventually looked forward to, but it was something astonishing, and long before his dream could have been half realised the system would have utterly outgrown any outside control. In the existing Universities the State Department finds it difficult enough to maintain the standard of examinations and degrees against the constant pressure of public opinion in the opposite direction. The general want is easy access to the great literate caste, to mount to which means the acquisition of a new social status, which carries withal the right of entry to all the sedentary employments. One would suppose that from a sense of vested interests those who have won their entry to the enclosure would be for keeping the gate to some extent against the growing throng outside; but it is not so, and on any and every occasion which involves the question public opinion is solid on the side of making the pass easier.

The craving for a degree, and, failing that, for the letters attached to the passing of one of the preliminary examinations which give the University stamp, must be largely founded on social ideas. In the East the man who sits on a chair has risen immeasurably above the manual worker. Education is respectability, from having been in the past the monopoly of Brahmans and bankers; conversely, for a low-caste fellow to aspire to it was formerly condemned as an invasion of the privileges of his betters. A friend of the writer sitting as a magistrate once had before him an elderly pundit who was charged with having committed a violent and apparently unprovoked assault on a coolie woman. His explanation was that he came upon her seated by the roadside reading the scriptures, and, scandalised by conduct so subversive of the gradations of society, had thought to correct the mischief with his cudgel. One can easily understand, then, the immense attractions that education holds out to boys of the

humbler classes: the prospect of mixing on
equal terms with youths of higher degree,
of qualifying like them for employment in
Government service, in the professions, in the
exalted order of clerkdom. No wonder every
father with a boy who has shown some promise
in the primary school should be ready to make
any sacrifice to start him on this ladder, on
which every rung is an examination which
brings the destruction of thousands of hopes.

But suppose the clever son of this humble
parent has climbed his way to the upper
flights and passed into a University, he will
find that, unfortunately, degrees are not a
livelihood, while thousands of those around
him are making the same discovery. A long
course of State Education has formed them
to the same mould, so that their desires and
difficulties are the same. The few professions
they can look to are already overcrowded,
and the law and medicine involve waiting;
teaching, which does not, is merely a synonym
for starvation, except for a very few bright
lights. Clerical employment, depressed by
the number of applicants, is miserably paid
also. No wonder that the thoughts of nine
out of ten of each year's educational outcrop
turn to Government service. Apart from any

other considerations, a Government billet has in their eyes a superior status to all other forms of employment; and though the lower and junior grades of the public services are not highly paid, the pay, combined with the security and the prospect of pension, is sufficient to make the opening intensely desirable in the eyes of the average graduate. The number of students attending the different Colleges now comes to above 45,000, of whom about 12,000 pass out into the world each year to seek their livelihood. Large though the number of appointments may be in the aggregate, only a small proportion of the total—say one in twenty—falls vacant annually, and this is nothing like sufficient to meet the wants of a throng that is always increasing.

Perhaps the extent to which this question of Government employment has come to possess and monopolise the minds of the middle class may be best illustrated by a personal experience. The writer's last holiday in India was a visit to a locality celebrated for its lakes and temples in the heart of the unadvanced Province of Bundelkund. On leaving the traveller's bungalow in the morning,

I found a cattle-fair in progress outside, and, stopping to look on, was soon joined by an elderly Mahomedan, a retired Inspector of Police, who was soon putting me through my paces. He knew, of course, that I was not one of the District Staff, but was I the Canal Officer? No, but probably I was on Land Settlement business? Still no; an Inspector of Education, then? Finally, I had to stand convicted of belonging to no office at all, which, he remarked regretfully, was a great pity, as he had a son to place, evidently believing that personal influence goes a long way in these matters, as it once did. In the afternoon the Tehsildar (sub-prefect) called to offer to drive me to a lake two or three miles away. He was a University man of the best class, a high-caste Hindu, a scholar and a gentleman, with a good knowledge of the local antiquities and a real feeling for the beauty of the scenery. He made a delightful guide, but it was evident that an oppression rested on his mind. It soon came out. The Government had taken to a new policy of making a certain number of Deputy-Collectorships (the grade above his own) by direct selection from University graduates who had passed well. This would, of course,

block the promotion of those who had entered
the service at the bottom, and he feared the
practice might extend. Could I throw any
light on this situation ? I gave him what
comfort I could, and we came back to the
sights; but he could not long shake off the
Deputy-Collectors, and was continually returning to them. I trust that by now he has
gained his promotion, for the service will not
lose thereby.

Next day was spent in a visit to the beau-
tiful headquarters of a Native State: water-
side palaces set in a natural park country
enclosed by low hills, a scene that might
have come straight from Todd's *Rajasthan*, a
specimen of the happy blending of landscape
and architectural beauties that gives these
gems of India their peculiar charm. Only
when the visitor finds himself in for a round
of inspection of the State educational institutions will he realise that the times are moving
even here. The special pride of the Minister
appeared to be the Industrial School, represented by a carpenter's bench and a loom with
the beginnings of a very commonplace carpet.
Sad to say, it was a holiday, and one could
not see the industries humming, but the existence of the place would show that the State

was in the movement. The Minister himself
had not much education, in the modern sense,
though evidently of abundant attainments
otherwise. But he had a son who was now
at college at Allahabad, getting near his
degree-time. Was he coming to the State
which had done so well under his father's
guidance ? No, he was for the British service;
if he did well in his examinations they might
hope for a Deputy-Collectorship.

My last experience of the courtesy of the
neighbourhood was when the station-master
lent me a chair in his room, the train being
late. Where was I going to ? Allahabad ?
He had a son in one of the high schools there,
but the boy would soon be going on to college.
And after college ? Why, it would depend
on how he did. A sub-Tehsildarship would
be fine, but it was looking high. Anyhow,
a Government post of some sort. Four con-
versations with totally different persons in
two days, and all had come round to the one
engrossing subject—the chances of a climb
into the abominated bureaucracy !

Naturally, the pressure on the portals where
so many desires meet is severe. Indian
feeling on the subject has become vociferous

during the last few years under the stimulus
imparted to it by the Public Services Commission, which, appointed in 1912, toured over
India during the two succeeding cold weathers,
took further evidence in England, and published its report last year; the full record of
the proceedings occupying twenty volumes.
The management of the inquiry took on a
popular character from the first, and high
hopes were raised in the Indian ranks by
what was known of the opinions of most of
its members. Actually it would not be
expected that such a large body, however
much it saturated itself with evidence, could
arrive at anything but compromises, and Lord
Islington achieved a remarkable feat in bringing his assortment of colleagues to agree in a
practically unanimous report. But this has
only been achieved by shunning the statement
of general guiding principles and avoiding some
stiff fences altogether. The Commission, in
short, has treated the subject empirically,
taking each branch of the Civil Services, small
or great, separately, and suggesting what
changes might be made in such matters as
its recruitment, numbers, pay, leave rules,
pensions, and the like. Nevertheless, it has
kept in view throughout the general object

of increasing the Indian element in every
branch, while the whole tone of the report is
manifestly favourable to Indian pretensions.
Where it has found any reason for the opinion
that a service should be transferred in due
course entirely to Indian agency, it has not
shrunk from recommending this; and few will
judge that it has not carried its liberality in
this matter to the furthest border of prudence.
But however that may be, the point is that
the proposals have utterly failed to satisfy
those whom it was hoped to please.

The commotion that was set up by the
Commission's sittings in India and the daily
evidence in the newspapers produced expectations that were growing all the while that the
report was held in abeyance, until by the
time it was allowed to appear its concessions
were scouted with one accord as utterly dis-
appointing and insufficient. European dissent
has, in fact, no reason for troubling to argue
its case, the Indian condemnation is so
emphatic. This was expressed in an un-
mistakable way in a long debate that took
place over the matter in the Viceroy's Legislative Council in the latter part of September
last, when not a single Indian member
apparently had a word to say in favour of the

Commission. This unlucky body had committed itself to the opinion that two branches of the Indian service, the Civil Service and the Police, must continue for general reasons to retain a preponderatingly European character. This audacious proposition has been treated on all hands as an affront to Indian feeling. As regards the Civil Service, the Commission recommended that for the future one quarter of the vacancies should be filled by appointments in India, while the Indian who chose would be as free as before to come to England and compete for the places offering by way of Burlington House. This adjustment was dismissed by the Simla debaters as totally inadequate. What will meet their demand (for the moment) is either that half the appointments should be given to India in the first instance, or that all should be thrown open to a competitive examination to be held simultaneously in India and England. Two or three speakers in the course of the discussion gave a clear indication that this would only be regarded as an instalment on account, and that an examination in India only, at which candidates from England might at first be allowed to compete, was the aim in view. If this would

Indianise the character of the Administration, they said it was no objection. It is time that it was Indianised.

If these are the sentiments of the selected few who reach the Viceregal Council, expressing themselves in that sedate atmosphere, it may be easily guessed how sentiments and language run in less enlightened quarters. As far as the question of a livelihood for the student population is concerned, the services are answering the purpose about as well as they can already. Practically all the posts it holds under the salary line of Rs. 200 a month—and few young men on starting can expect more—are held by Indians. The total number of posts to which salaries above this figure attach is in round numbers 11,000, of which 42 per cent. are held by Indians. As the scale rises, the proportion of this holding decreases, until in the class of incomes of Rs. 800 per month and over it falls to 10 per cent. If this seems small, it must be looked at beside the fact that in 1887, when the question was last overhauled, the percentage was only 4. But these higher appointments do not touch the college population, whose case would not be appreciably alleviated if

all of them were from this time forth reserved
to their countrymen. No consideration of
the question, moreover, can admit the immense
change that has come about since 1887 in the
practice of appointing Indians to the very
highest posts—to the Secretary of State's
Council, the Governor-General's Council, the
Executive Councils in the major Provinces,
the High Court benches, innovations which
in many cases have notoriously been attended
by the difficulty of finding any suitable person
to nominate for the important positions thus
thrown open, and which, nevertheless, have
not produced the smallest effect of satisfaction
to moderate the general tone of discontent.
For behind any small class which concessions
can affect comes that body of ill-will, solidified
by a common system of education, which,
Anglicised in its expression, Asiatic at heart,
envies and detests us, and is bent on using
any means which we put in its way of clearing
us out of the country.

CHAPTER VI

THE FORGOTTEN EUROPEAN

ONE comes now to a branch of the subject which has to be introduced to the reader's attention with a sense of delicacy and diffidence, it being contrary to the way of Secretaries of State and Viceroys and other luminaries to whom we look for guidance to recognise that it calls for any consideration whatsoever—the European element, official and non-official. The interests of this community have been so overlaid of recent times by the "ideals" and "aspirations" of others, that there would seem to be something reactionary, invidious, immoral almost, in dwelling upon the fact that they even exist. Nevertheless, as the British element is still there, and as it is beyond any question that they alone have made the country what it is to-day, it is inevitable that any political settlement in which they are ignored will pay the penalty of the oversight as the scheme comes into working.

Instinctively, we are most of us inclined to believe that there must be a moral force at work behind every great achievement in history, the vital principle which was destined to carry the movement on and through. Yet it must be owned that this is difficult to discover in the beginnings of the British Indian Empire. The humble traders who found themselves engaged at so much disadvantage on an Indian career in their scattered warehouse settlements along the coast, separated from each other hardly less than from Europe—what accounts for the desperate tenacity with which they clung to their precarious holdings ? They did not dream of territory; they could hardly be said to be working for their own advantage, for they were miserably paid and provided, and what profits they could make by pushing trade went to their employers at home. What voice was in their minds telling them to hang on to their calicoes, muslins, and sandalwoods in spite of Nawabs, Rajas, and pirates ? From the first they have to sue the country Powers for leave to trade and exist; gradually they are led to take a hand in country politics for their own better security. Then the soldier appears on the scene, in the shape of a company or two of sepoys, with a score of Europeans to do the drill and man the Fort's guns. In due course these garrisons grow to field forces. A great Frenchman next arrives on the scene, who develops this military system immensely and begins to have a clear vision of a Southern Indian Empire; but the merchants of Fort St. George and Fort St. David, who were very near to being extinguished by him, did not enter into his ambitions, and blessed the day when he fell into disgrace with his own Government. As for the soldiery of these little armies that marched up and down the Carnatic, men drawn to the martial profession mostly by the agency of the press-gang, what can have mattered less to them than the merits of a difference between Chunda Sahib and Mahomet Ali ? Nevertheless, these makers of Empire, badly paid, provisioned chiefly on rice and arrack, campaigning in an abominable climate, fought when they encountered the French like tigers, as the casualty rolls remain to prove.

Then comes the day when one of the rush-lights of Empire is blown out. The news arrives at Madras that Fort William has been captured by the Nawab of Bengal, and that after a shocking atrocity the remnant of

Calcutta residents are refugees on a festering mud-flat at the mouth of the Hooghly. The story of the consequent events—the expedition of Clive and Watson, the recovery of Calcutta, the Battle of Plassey, the flight and death of Suraj-ud-Dowlah, and the transfer of Bengal—is so dramatic, so improving, that it must have been seized upon in school histories as an illustration of the working of Providence and of the inevitable retribution that awaits such acts as the Black Hole massacre. But as we are looking at the fortuitous side of the phenomenon of British development, it may be pointed out that this version is open to serious exceptions. The sailing of Clive and Watson for Bengal was an accident due to the belated news of the declaration of the Seven Years' War. Had a state of hostilities with Pondicherry set in, Madras could not have afforded to send troops to Bengal. The Battle of Plassey was in no way fought to avenge the Black Hole. Clive's aims were met by the retaking of Fort William, and as soon as that was achieved peace was concluded with the Nawab. What brought about the campaign of Plassey was the subsequent intrigues of Suraj-ud-Dowlah with the French, and the heavy fight of the campaign was with the French at their settlement of Chandernagore. Plassey was in no sense a decisive victory, as another and much more severely contested action had to be fought almost on the same field a year later; nor did Plassey " secure Bengal for England," as I find stated in an excellent little reference history of England before me. Bengal was not secured until eight years later, a period crowded with more fighting, new combinations, vicissitudes of every kind, during which at almost any moment things might have gone differently, taking a turn which would have changed the whole course of subsequent events. The philosopher, wise after the event, may be able to run a thread of theory through all this strange, eventful history; but the psychologist appears to be on firmer ground when he sees nothing but the innate qualities of the higher race continually asserting themselves at every crisis over every obstacle.

It was the grant of Bengal and Behar that settled the permanency of the connection between Britain and India, but let it be recalled that this acquisition was no act of violence. There was, in fact, a strong feeling

among the Company's people in India as well
as England against launching out into the
responsibilities of territorial government, and
the Emperor's offer was declined in the first
instance, and only accepted after the experiment of governing by Indian agency had
proved quite impracticable. The period
between the death of Suraj-ud-Dowlah and
the acceptance of the Dewani saw in effect a
trial of the policy of "association," and the
result was an absolute failure. What the
Emperor parted with was the revenue and
administration of two provinces which
had been virtually independent, receiving in
return a tribute which he might now expect
would henceforth take the form of cash
instead of flowery acknowledgments of respect
and devotion. But a few years later the
Emperor himself was carried off prisoner by
the Mahrattas, and the Company's sovereignty
became absolute. Anchored to the country
by the possession of Bengal, the Company's
position was no longer liable to extinction
by a gust of adversity, and when in 1769 it
seemed probable that Madras might suffer
the same fate at the hands of Hyder
as Calcutta in 1757, the hazard was not
so extreme as it would have been if the

Mysorean had come to the top a decade or two earlier.

Meanwhile, the Writers and Factors of Bengal had been suddenly transformed into Governors, while their morale had been sapped by the confusion of the interregnum and the lucrative opportunities of Nawab - making. The smoke of Macaulay's heavy guns still hangs over this period, and no doubt it was a disreputable and greedy one. But, nevertheless, the British spirit was at work all the time. The men who fleeced the Nawabs and Viziers were no sooner Governors than they began to think of the condition of the people. The first general memorandum on Bengal Land Revenue Administration is a wonderful State paper to have been the production of men new to the subject. There are, moreover, ideas in it of which no Native Government hitherto has ever dreamed. It is a worthy foundation for a branch of Government to which many of the best minds of each succeeding generation of Anglo-Indians will devote the best part of their lives, a work bringing incalculable benefits to the country and to the people— directly affecting the internal relations of an enormous landed society, indirectly affecting the entire community. Land revenue business

in its details is hard and intricate, demanding
work in the field in actual contact with the
people as much as in the office. Perhaps
there is no better embodiment possible of the
life and labours of the Revenue service than
the figure of its first expert, Sir Thomas
Munro, as, taking off his uniform, he goes
down to Canara, to sit from morning to night
in his tent surrounded by crowds of the natives
examining their titles and registers and draw-
ing out of them the realities of the land system
of a then unknown country, only interrupting
his work to correspond with Colonel Arthur
Wellesley, who is campaigning on the other
side of the hills. The name of this truly great
man is still remembered, as it deserves,
throughout Southern India; but in general
those who follow him have little to expect in
the way of fame, the work being too technical
for general appreciation. Thus, though no
men have done more for the country than
those who have achieved a good settlement
of a district, the merits of the accomplishment are only understood by a few officers of
their own service.

The very success of the work done for
India in the management of the land question

has helped to put it out of recognition, the
subject never being heard of except when
some piece of agrarian legislation rouses a
controversy. To appreciate the significance
of this preponderating interest, the best way
is, perhaps, to take a glimpse of what happens
when things go amiss with this branch of
administration or the subject is neglected.
Not to go back to the records of pre-British
days, let us take the case of the Bombay
Presidency, which had no Munro to lay the
beginnings of a land revenue school. Sir
Bartle Frere, during his Governorship, had
occasion in 1864 to introduce a Land Survey
and Settlement Bill, and in doing so he gave
his Council a remarkable experience.

> Nearly thirty years had passed, he said, since
> he was personally connected with the operations
> which led to the commencement of the Survey
> in that Presidency, and was himself employed
> in the districts in which the Survey was first
> introduced. It was impossible to give anyone
> who had not seen the country at the time he
> was speaking of an idea of how this India, which
> is always said to be immutable, had changed
> for the better, and how much of that change
> was due to one good measure of administration,
> steadily and consistently carried out. The
> situation was shortly this: Rarely more than

two-thirds of the culturable land in any district was under cultivation; frequently as much as two-thirds of the land was waste. Villages almost deserted were frequently to be met with. Some were *bè chiragh*, without a light in them, utterly uninhabited. The people were sunk in the lowest depths of poverty; they had few recognised rights in the land. The rates were so much higher than could possibly be paid at the existing prices of produce that it was necessary to grant remissions, of the necessity and extent of which the local (Native) officers were the sole judges; and it was thus left practically to a very ill-paid class of inferior Native officials to decide what was to be taken from the people. . . .

Bare figures could not describe the progress that had been made in any district where the Survey rates of assessment had been long in operation. Cultivation had been increased to a truly remarkable extent, so much so that he believed it would be a difficult matter now to find anywhere, in the Deccan area, a thousand acres of unoccupied cultivable land available for anyone wishing to take up land for cultivation. Land was not only occupied, but valued.*

The Land Revenue officer who has seen such changes may see and be satisfied with the travail of his soul. It needs no reflection

* Proceedings of Bombay Council, October 18, 1864.

to realise what chances a population in the state recalled by Sir Bartle Frere would have stood against the arrival of famine. It would not be true to say that the Native Governments cared nothing for famine; they cared a great deal for it—as affecting their own revenues. In justice it must be said that none of the country Governments after the Moghul Empire had commenced to decline had the means for attempting to grapple with such a visitation as a famine, but the revenue regulations in Bengal, designed for squeezing the last rupee out of a ruined society, betray an incredible callousness to any consideration but the ruler's income.

The Company's servants, long after they had entered on the work of government, had to look on helplessly, and shocking even at this distance are the accounts of what the spectacle of a famine in the old time meant, the skeleton host in its migrations being followed by packs of wolves and jackals, which bred on the calamity, as the mice breed to-day on our Government's wheat stores in Australia. But about the time which Sir Bartle Frere was describing above, the beginnings of a policy of famine protection were being laid in the United Provinces by Colonel

Baird Smith, afterwards to be known to the
world as Chief Engineer at the Siege of Delhi.
Still, whatever might be done locally in the
way of canals and grain stores, the country
could not be assured against famine mortality
until the day when it should be completely
covered by a system of railways.   Even then
it would be terribly difficult to bring adequate
help to a people such as those of Sir Bartle
Frere's description, half starved at the outset.
The great defence against famine is a rise in
the standard of living among the people.   This
country, even in the days when it drew no
supplies from abroad, seems never to have
suffered from actual famine.   The reason is
expressed in the saying that the English lived
upon wheat, while the Irish lived upon
potatoes: in other words, the people that
subsists upon the higher level in ordinary
times has the larger margin to fall back upon
in the day of adversity.

That the Indian population generally has
begun to rise above the danger line is clearly
enough shown by the experience of the last
famine period.   Between 1896 and 1910 India
was subjected to no less than four of these
disastrous visitations of the first or second
magnitude.   In former times such an accu-

mulation of calamities must have had results
that would have left their mark on the face of
the country and on its economy for a quarter
of a century. Actually we are confronted
with this extraordinary result, that the last
of the series was the least felt of all the four.
Rapidly rising prosperity, judicious land laws,
a cheap Government and light taxation, an
Administration in the hands of able men
thoroughly in sympathy with the people,
knowing precisely what measures are required
in the way of suspensions of revenue, money
advances, help with seed or cattle, and so on,
and prepared to act at once—there is the
secret. The land is the master interest in
India, and to have freed it from the grip of
famine while ensuring that the 230 millions
or so whose existence is directly bound up
with it shall live their lives interfered with
and taxed as little as possible, and with as
little friction as possible between landholder
and tenant—this is an achievement that need
not make Britain blush for the representatives
who have been doing her work, and deserves
to be described in some history more appetising
than the Blue books.

In truth, there is something radically
absurd in the spectacle of the British Govern-

ment being placed on its trial at the instance of a public which has done nothing for itself, and has even derived all the ideas and doctrine which furnish the act of accusation from the very Administration that it arraigns. There is a class of philosophic mind that sees in every present discontent the consequence of some far-off wrong, as the present mood of Ireland is attributed to Elizabeth and Cromwell, or agrarian troubles to the rankling effects of the Statute of Labourers or the enclosure of commons in minds that know nothing of either. The wildest of this school has never pretended that Indian unrest springs from the short-lived misdoings of the predatory Bengal Nabobs. The Company's Government was, in fact, from the moment it was fairly established, an infinitely better Government than the country had ever known, and it contained within itself the principle of improvement, when every good Native Government that had preceded it contained only the seeds of decline. On this point let the reader take the testimony of James Mill, that harsh judge, who in his history of British India has contrived to be equally unfair to British and Indians, but who, nevertheless, in summary could write of the Company's rule thus:

Mill † In matters of detail I have more frequently had occasion to blame the Company's Government than to praise it; and till the business of government is much better understood, whoever writes history, with a view solely to the good of mankind, will have the same thankless task to perform; yet I believe it will be found that the Company during the period of their sovereignty have done more in behalf of their subjects, have shown more goodwill towards them, have shown less of a selfish attachment to mischievous powers lodged in their own hands, have displayed a more generous welcome to schemes of improvement, and are now more willing to adopt improvements, not only than any other Sovereign existing in the same period, but than all Sovereigns taken together upon the surface of the globe.

The worst thing that can be said about the Company's Government in its latter days is that it was backward in its attitude towards the furthering of material improvements, and no doubt the original antagonism between the service and outsiders left its trace in a reluctance to measures involving an appeal to British enterprise and capital. But the position of the old Government was not so strong politically as it became after the Crown took over charge, and there may have been reasons to apprehend that a free inflow of capital—as, for instance, for canal construction—might bring some danger to public interests. In the country itself there certainly was no capital to be enlisted in the pre-Mutiny period, the beginnings of Indian wealth in the modern sense having dated from the American Civil War, just as clearly as the second access of prosperity in these latter days dates from the development of the South African mines and the consequent fall in the value of gold, which raised the prices of all Indian produce and has kept them rising. "That Minister is clever," says an old Eastern saw, "who, without putting his hand on anyone's head, can increase the Treasury;" but this is what the Indian Finance Ministers of the current century have been able to do. Money has been found in abundance for education, sanitation, and for the questionable luxury of new capitals, while the only tax paid by the poor, the salt duty, has been largely reduced. And not merely this, but the State has suffered the loss of the opium revenue, which would have wrecked the finances of the sixties and seventies outright, and has been able to accommodate itself to the disappearance without being put to

deficit or dislocation. There could be no
stronger evidence than this remarkable fact
of the general prosperity of the country, as
well as the excellence of that branch of the
Administration on whose management all the
others depend.

But, indeed, if we take James Mills's criterion
of looking at the subject solely with an eye to
the good of mankind, the Government of
India is entitled to a very high place among
the Governments of the world. In many
respects the Administration is far in advance
of European standards. If a person were to
go through the State papers published in the
Government *Gazette*, which in India go under
the title of Resolutions, beginning from thirty
or forty years ago, he would have no difficulty
in compiling a manual of administration which
any other Government might learn much from.
The machinery of Government wanted no
improving—at least, in any respect within
the comprehension of the people—and has not
been in the smallest degree improved by the
Council-Parliaments of 1909, which are a
clumsy, inefficient device as far as the working goes, whatever their counteracting merits
may be.

But until the Montagu millennium comes

in, the important thing in Indian administration will be to prevent the gulf which necessarily exists between the Government and
the people from widening. This is the work
of the British officer, for the Indian sub-
ordinate officials of the Revenue or Police by
whom everyday contact is maintained naturally do not count. And who can say that the
men who have had this work to do have failed
in their task ? There is a passage of quite
surprising foolishness in the Public Service
Commission's Report on the educational qualifications of the Civilian of the future, suggesting that a combination of the attainments
of Mountstuart Elphinstone, Mackintosh, and
Colonel Henry Yule, might about do to start
with. And the wonderful beings who come
up to the mark are to load themselves with
learning that they may come out, formed
men, to begin on the trial of petty criminality,
with the consciousness that their future
career is well overcast with the possibility of
political changes. It is a matter of notoriety
that already among the younger men in the
services the common expression in discussing
these subjects, "The thing will last out our
time," has changed to " Will it last out our
time ?" The likelihood of that is seen differ-

ently by different persons, but it is idle to think of catching brilliant men, or that, if caught, their powers will come to fruition, if they are to become the servants of the public in the sense joyously anticipated by the Indian agitator. The best men of the Haileybury and Addiscombe age, and those of the day of pure nomination which preceded, became what they were, not by virtue of the book learning they started with, but because early responsibilities and important employments drew out their natural powers, whether for governing, diplomacy, engineering, public economy, science, or research. The way in which many of them oftentimes made names in the active life and the studious equally speaks to the virtue of opportunity.

The times, of course, have changed, and it is no longer possible that the many-sided career should fall to any individual. But the British officer remains what he was, and is still the power that is taking the country along. To realise what he is it is necessary to have seen the District Magistrate in his camp in the mango-grove, where, with the aid of two or three clerks somewhere in the background, and a few mounted constables or camel sowars to maintain communications with his capital, he manages the concerns of a population of perhaps a million people, whose local representatives will throng his door from morning to night. Somewhere else in his domain may be the similar camps of the Assistant Magistrate and of the Police Superintendent. These three, with perhaps a judge and doctor at the headquarters, are responsible for maintaining the British character of the administration over an area of perhaps 4,000 square miles, and it may be judged whether they are not at the service of the public in the fullest sense of the term. Other pictures of the work that is being done by the guidance of the few and the hands of the multitude may be seen at the building of a big bridge, where the whole of the science that is fighting the obstacles of Nature is represented by the temporary quarters of the two engineers in charge, or at a large famine work.

Perhaps the most impressive scene of all in this sort within the writer's experience was on the lofty crest of the Khoja Amran range looking out over the camel-coloured desert of the Kandahar plain, up to which the railway had been pushed all the way from the Indus valley in the face of frightful difficulties of ground and climate, till now the end had been reached, and it only remained to pierce the range with a tunnel which would carry the rails down to the terminus below, the starting-point in case of an extension into Afghanistan. A large camp settlement had sprung up at the tunnel-head. In this desert all the thousands of Pathan labourers had to be maintained, hutted, and, not least, kept in order. And this great enterprise, so singularly impressive in the solitudes of a rugged wilderness, was entirely in the hands of half a dozen young engineers, mostly civilians, their chief a Brunel of barely middle age. He would have been a strange man who spent a day at that mess without feeling prouder of his country-men; and when the charge is made against the Anglo-Indian official that he is wanting in understanding and sympathy it may be asked how the existence of those qualities could be better shown than by scenes such as those above glanced at, and many another instance might be added—the relations of the officers of the Native Army to their men, the relations of Chiefs and Politicals. But un-doubtedly the English official is not a demo-cratic phenomenon; for democracy is a force in which, in theory at least, the majesty of the mass involves the insignificance of the individual. Whether or not the democratic theory can ever work out true, or will merely lead to the concentration of power in a few under a veil of forms and references, it is certain that the Anglo-Indian officer cannot be reduced to insignificance. He must either direct or go; and although there are many Indians now in the service who are doing the same work as their confrères, they succeed because of their place in an established system. If we imagine the English withdrawn and their system to remain, it could not long retain its efficiency on the force of memory and imitation; while an Indian bureaucracy under control of an Assembly or Assemblies would infallibly mean an immediate descent into misgovernment, until bottom had been touched at the level of Persia.

CHAPTER VII

ANOTHER IMPEDIMENT—THE NON-OFFICIAL

Race pop in India

IT appears that in the year preceding the war the number of British Europeans in India amounted to 178,000. Deducting from this some 75,000 British soldiers, with 15,000 more to represent their wives and families, the officials, and the probably still larger number of persons of mixed descent now absurdly christened "Anglo-Indians" for the sake of importing confusion into plain meanings, who may have preferred to enter themselves as belonging to Europe, the total is not a large one for the representatives of the ruling race in a country reaching from the Hindu Kush to the borders of Siam and China. The smallness of numbers in itself points to the fact that there is no settlement on the land among the English, the private person no less than the official having in mind from the day of arrival the thought of the ship which will eventually carry him away. Small and scattered over such a surface of country, this community is not in a good way of making its influence felt; but the part it has played in having brought the country to its present state of development is out of all proportion to its numbers, and what it has done has certainly been achieved with a minimum of encouragement or assistance. For a brief period, the ten or fifteen years following the Mutiny, the fostering of a permanent European element of settlers was in some favour, and land grants in the sub-Himalayan regions, improved schooling, and openings for the children of the long-service British soldier, were ideas in vogue. But they soon passed, and it was as well that they did, for experience amply shows that the Anglo-Indian (proper) has no abiding-place in India, and that it is wrong kindness to give him inducements to stay.

Putting apart, then, the small body of settlers, the British community outside the service consists practically entirely of persons engaged in commerce, the industries, planting, and the railway. Except for the cotton-mill system of Western India, the keys of all the important businesses of the country are in their hands, and the business is mostly of their creation. The tea trade, the jute trade, indigo so long as it lasted, coal-mining, gold-mining, shipping, and in these latter days the promotion of feeder lines of railways, electric light supply schemes, and finally the banking system that operates the whole, are practically the creation of the migratory Anglo-Indian. In doing this great work for the country it certainly cannot be said that he has met with any undue encouragement from his own Government. The East India Company was always apprehensive of the appearance of any large interests backed by British capital between itself and its subjects, and the tradition passed on to the succeeding Administration, which early in its day declared war with the one great European industry that had yet grown up, the indigo planting of Bengal. This is not the place for the venturing of any opinion on that great controversy, for the final blow to indigo was to come from another quarter, the aniline dyes of Germany; but it may be said that the Government must have often had reason lately to regret the disappearance of that fine body of British volunteer cavalry formerly furnished by the planting community who, knowing the country and people perfectly, could be trusted to maintain order in the ungarrisoned districts of Behar and Bhaugulpore.

Another industry which, though on a very much smaller scale, must often be regretted in these last times is the breweries. Encouraged in its early days by the Government for the sake of having at hand an independent source of supply for the troops, the policy in Lord Kitchener's time was harshly reversed, with the result that, the army demands being the mainstay of the trade, one brewery after another had to close down. The remnant still left in existence when the war broke out must be put to it to meet the situation now, and one suspects that a good deal of hardship has been inflicted on troops and public worse than needlessly. Had the industry been in different hands there would have been an uproar. But the Government knew that the Anglo-Indian owner and shareholder would do nothing more than grumble inaudibly, so it followed out its own inclination. .Another Anglo-Indian industry that has gone downhill of late years is the coffee-planting of Southern India, which twenty-five years ago, after disease had ruined the flourishing plantations of Ceylon, seemed for a time to have a brilliant future before it.

The disappointment of this hope was due to the increased competition of South America, which nothing would have helped short of a differential treatment in the British market; but when the Government can give the industry in its declined state a little cut of unkindness, it generally seems to be glad to do so. Still, the European community holds its own, and manages to maintain its position and usefulness to the country in spite of such reverses.

The enormous growth of the tea trade and the establishment of the coal trade have obliterated any set-backs at other points, and the general growth in the production and wealth of the country has brought increase of business to all who are concerned in the moving of exports and imports in its various ramifications. Also, they have brought a great increase to the retail trade, which stands on a peculiar footing in India, where there is not that sharp line between the shop and the warehouse or manufactory that exists in England. The wholesale importer of Calcutta will often advertise his willingness to sell you a dozen of claret or whisky; on the other hand, it is impossible to consider the head of a great retail establishment which may be called on to send out an electric light installation to Kabul, or a printing press to Bhutan, together with the artificers to set up the plant and teach its use, as on a level with the ordinary tradesman of Europe.

Some of the heads of these large firms in Calcutta or Bombay have the income of merchant princes; they may not be often found in the Bengal or Byculla Club, but meet one of them in private life and you may easily discover a better educated person than yourself. After all, it is not astonishing that the social level in such a community as the Europeans of Calcutta or Rangoon should be high. "The economical advantages of commerce," says John Stuart Mill, "are surpassed in importance by those of its effects which are intellectual and moral. It is hardly possible to overrate the value, in the present low state of human improvement, of placing human beings in contact with persons dissimilar to themselves, and with modes of thought and action unlike those with which they are familiar." One is tempted to wonder whether that generalisation was suggested to his mind by his interviews with returned men of business at the India House; but in any case the Associated Tradesmen of Anglo-

India are a body who can afford to hold their heads high.

It is necessary to keep in mind that the non-official, European community, for all practical purposes, is represented by the business communities of the three Presidency towns, and that of these the Calcutta congregation is by far the most important. Outside these centres one may find Chambers of Commerce and various Associations with long titles and small memberships, but they are too few and scattered to count towards large issues in their several capacities. They usefully represent important provincial interests; but politically, if they wish to say anything, they must say ditto to Calcutta, in which there is no harm, the political interests of Anglo-Indians all over India being identical. Now, as long as the Government made Calcutta its winter headquarters, Anglo-Indian opinion was able to exercise informally its due influence on the Government. It may be allowed that Calcutta in the strength of its position was frequently, like the Labourites to-day, unnecessarily truculent and aggressive in the expression of its sentiments, and the ebullition in which it annually indulged

over the Government migration to the hills
was a local extravagance, no outside opinion
craving that the Government of India should
be tied the whole year round to Calcutta.
But it remains a fact that the connection
with Calcutta did enable the Anglo-Indian
view of public questions to be presented with
due weight to the Government, and the real
power which this opinion could bring into
action on occasion was revealed in the Ilbert
Bill collision. To-day there is no effectual
means of focussing the remonstrances of an
indignant community; but the strength of
the great agitation against Lord Ripon's
measure lay, not in the fact that the cheers
of the indignation meeting of 1883 pene-
trated through the windows of Government
House, but that more than half of the officials
belonging to the Government of India itself
had notoriously by that time been convinced
that the Viceroy was in the wrong.

This could not happen now. Since the
removal to Delhi the Government of India no
longer comes into contact with outside European opinion at all, and this has already
modified its character with extraordinary
rapidity, considering the few years that the
change has been in effect. A considerable

portion of its members appear to have thought
that with the new régime it behoved them to
thrust authority out of sight and to put on
the garb of the supple, contriving politician.
Intent on effecting this change of costume,
they have succumbed to the influences they
meant to take charge of. In the quietude of
Delhi and Simla the debating in the Legislative Council has come to assume an exag-
gerated importance in the eyes of the small
centre circle of official life. The thirty or
forty Indian Councillors and journalists who
appear at headquarters in connection with
the meetings are the only public of which
the members of the Government see much
at close quarters, and with whose opinions
and views they stand much chance of being
impressed. The consequence is a great
accretion in the importance of the class
of questions which the non-official Councillors particularly cultivate, and a drop in
the prominence of those with which they
are not concerned. The same tendency is at
work in the Provincial Councils, but much
less distortingly, because the Provincial
Governments are in touch with their publics
in every direction at first hand. But in all
this influence acquired over the Government

by the quasi-representative system the European element have no share, and by so much has their position deteriorated, for no fault of their own.

To appreciate how much the position has turned against them, it is only necessary to go back to the days before 1892, when the Additional Members were selected by direct nomination. At that time the Government, knowing no politics, took things as it found them, and simply chose the men who were marked out as most representative of substantial interests, and most likely to be of assistance for practical purposes to the work of the Council. Under this system two or three of the leading members of the Calcutta Bar, including, I think, invariably, the Advocate-General of Bengal, as well as two or three of the leading men of the business world, were taken up each season into the legislature. These outside members brought a fresh mind to public affairs, which was of real advantage to their official colleagues, and the lawyer members especially were of high value to a Government which has little assistance to fall back upon in this regard. When controversial questions arose, the debates were on a far higher level than those of to-day, notably in the matter of financial criticism, as anyone can convince himself by turning back to the Reports of the Council proceedings of that period.

What is the position now ? The Council has been trebled in numbers, while the representation of the entire European community is confined to the two members who sit for the Chambers of Commerce of Calcutta and Bombay respectively, the latter of whom, it may be said, would never be chosen by the general voice, since the Bombay business world has a peculiar character all its own, and its chief is often a man who is totally unknown to the public at large. To the domiciled Europeans and Eurasians a member has been allowed, but when the infinitely more important European community asked for the same privilege they were told that it was impossible, for the reason that it would involve an additional seat. In spite of this convincing objection, the Association in which they have been driven to combine to defend their interests, and which has a larger membership merely as a matter of numbers than any existing constituency in the Imperial Council, is still asking for this one member, but apparently without any prospect of success.

In the writer's opinion, it makes a mistake in continuing to press the matter, since an isolated European non-official could do no more than put in an occasional forlorn protest, while his absence is eloquent testimony to the hollowness and irrationality of the representative system in its Indian application.

In general, the European community has not greatly troubled about the prejudicing of its position by experiments in representation. Its reliance has been in the integrity and impartiality of its Government, and even when clashes occurred, as over the indigo question, the suffering interest could appreciate the motives that made it decide against them. In the long run men felt that a Government that stood for equal justice to all classes could be trusted with the cause of its countrymen, even if the very desire to be fair sometimes gave it an unconscious bias. It is only of late years, since it has seen the Government deteriorating and acknowledging expediency and the desire for the favour of particular classes as motives for action, that the British non-official world has in spite of itself been driven to combination and protests. On the other hand, if the Europeans

10

have lost faith in their Government, the Government has given the best proof that it has not ceased to rely upon them. As the war had drained the country of every British soldier who could possibly be spared, the Government was forced to be anxious about the internal situation. The loyalty of the people of India was splendid, but there was too much opportunity for the development of emotions of another sort.

For some six weeks of the late autumn of 1914, between the departure of four-fifths of the British garrison and the arrival of the Territorials, the maintenance of British rule rested largely upon the shoulders of the Volunteers, Europeans and Eurasians. This body, numbering about 40,000 in all, were willing enough, but in a rudimentary state as regards organisation, training, equipment, and disciplinary powers. More was required, and early last year came the order for the formation of the Indian Defence Force. The average Britisher has probably never yet realised that compulsory military service is now in force in India, as far as his own countrymen are concerned, but this is the case. The Defence Force takes in every individual of the community between the ages of eighteen and forty-one, while the older men are caught up by the Act into a sort of Landsturm, not required to serve beyond local limits. Otherwise the whole force is subject to military discipline, has to undergo a prescribed training locally, followed by a couple of months' course at some military centre, which may be in a distant part of the country, and at the end is liable for service in any part of India. The introduction of the system was bound to bear very hardly on Anglo-India, where such a thing as an unoccupied man of military age is unknown, and where the system, whether of Government or of private establishments, is to work with a minimum of Europeans in the control posts, who are therefore almost indispensable.

Outside half a dozen big centres, moreover, the Europeans are scattered over the country in diminutive communities, altogether too small for military purposes. The man at a little station, therefore, has had to move to a larger one, even for his preliminary training, submitting to all the inconvenience of such a change; but the hardest case of all, probably, is that of the planter, who, sole manager of his own garden, and probably that of his next-door neighbour departed for the army, is haled off to the Defence Force, leaving the concern to Providence and a jemedar.

According to all accounts, the Defence Force Act has been so worked from Simla as to bring about the maximum of hardship to individuals with the least effect; but be that as it may, the burdens which have fallen on magistrates and judges, clerks and commercial travellers, impartially, would not have been endured in vain if there was any hope that they would teach the rulers and the British public generally how indisputably the European element is the backbone of the Indian Empire. To make the fact more staring is the contrast of the Indian branch of the Defence Force. For thirty years the National Congress had been annually affirming the inherent right of an Indian to bear arms for his own country; so to meet the pent-up demand the Government, while it was introducing compulsory service for Europeans, announced the creation of a Volunteer Defence Force for Indians, stipulating that the numbers should be limited to 6,000 until the training machinery could be expanded to meet the expected inrush. Some time after, when the results were announced, it appeared that the recruits

numbered about 300. Finally, after great
exertions and drum-beating on the part of
the people's leaders the list has been closed
down on a total roll of about 5,000, which is
a sufficient comment on the reality of the
passionate aspirations after military service
in the defence of the country of which so
much was heard until the door was opened.

To turn to another side of life. No survey
of the European position in India ought to
overlook the missionary element, which, however, generally is overlooked. The Company,
always very tender on the subject of Indian
sentiment, delighted to show its impartiality
by repressive measures against the early
missionaries, while its own chaplains could
be safely trusted not to light the brand of
religious enthusiasm. Gradually the missionaries worked their way to toleration, and,
inspired by the evangelicism of the day, began
to foresee the time at hand when the printing
press and the spread of education must bring
about the speedy collapse of heathenism.
The movement then came to encounter a new
opposition, with its headquarters in Liberal
opinion in England, and from Sydney Smith
to Matthew Arnold its designs against the

religion of the country were subjected to a galling fire of banter, in which the Anglo-Indian Press freely joined. That standing antagonism within the last couple of decades has completely died down, principally because the movement itself has changed direction. The missionary, in fact, though he does not say so, has almost ceased to seek to proselytise. The Indian Christian population numbers now above three and a half millions, and a body of this size naturally shows appreciable growth decade by decade by the natural process of increase within its own ranks. But of this total over two millions are returned as absolutely uneducated, showing that the immense majority belong to the depressed classes, people whose conversion could never have been regarded as the spoiling of a Hindu.

For the rest, the missionary of to-day may be a physician, fruit-farmer, dairyman, poultry-raiser, or anything useful, but in the majority of instances he is an educationist pure and simple. It is in his schools and colleges that he comes into contact with Indians of the better classes; but the aim of conversion has to be kept in the background, for if it came to be successful it would empty the institutions. So he ploughs his lonely

furrow content to do good indirectly by
influence, holding himself aloof even in the
mofussil from European society and its
interests, without entering much into the
minds of the people. Yet all the time the
zeal of his supporters at home does not seem
to lessen, and up to the outbreak of the war,
while Government improvements might be
held up for shortness of funds, the missionary,
and especially the American missionary, never
seemed to fail for resources to carry out any
extensions that he had in view. There is
probably no means of arriving at what the
different missionary bodies spend each year
in India, much less at what they have laid
out in the aggregate during the century that
they have been at work, but it must be a vast
sum. Against the European official it may
be said (though it is a poor-spirited sort of
argument) that even if he supplies the good
administration that has created the wealth
of to-day, he sends some portion of his salary
to England, and his pension has to be paid
in England, and that in this respect his
emoluments are a drain on the country. But
at any rate the missionary stands economi-
cally on irreproachable ground. His small
salary and such retiring allowances as he may

enjoy are paid throughout by those who send him, and the amount that he manages to procure for the building and service of colleges, schools, hospitals, rural dispensaries, training farms, and so forth, is all net gain to the country.   There can hardly be another such instance of sustained philanthropic endeavour as this tide of benefaction and benevolence which has flowed from West to East during the past century, sad to say without producing any commensurate results even in the creation of ordinary goodwill.   But the effort is not a thing to be ignored in taking account of the relations between the countries, and the position which the missionaries have acquired is one that entitles them, merely on secular grounds, to be considered before coming to a political settlement which might imperil their footing in the country.

A more singular position, indeed, was never contrived by political perversity than this which the new reform scheme contemplates for the European element in India.   The first thing that any person of any part of the world has in mind, and cannot help having in mind, when he thinks of modern India is of a country which is what it is by virtue of the British connection.   Under   whatever   aspect   its current affairs and conditions are looked at, everything comes back to a British source. The term "British India" does not merely express a territorial sovereignty, for by this time it may be broadly said that there is no India that is not British. The sojourners who represent the potent, transforming energy of the ruling country are few in numbers, but very strong in position and influence. They represent all the driving force in every department of administrative activity, in material progress and enterprise, and they have, too, the moral strength that comes from being the representatives of a civilisation which the Indians, in proportion as they advance, set themselves to imitate, down to the adoption of their speech as a common language for the educated. And in face of these conditions we are setting ourselves to devise a political system in which this predominant community is to be simply set aside; in which one section, the officials (as long as they are retained), will be voiceless, as belonging to the public service; and the other, because of the fewness of its numbers, can never be represented in any real sense of the term. An arrangement that begins by doing such flagrant violence to the realities, how can it be expected to work ?

CHAPTER VIII

THE POLICY OF ASSOCIATION

WHEN reformers of the school of Montagu speak to us of changes delicately described as "tending in the direction of self-government," it is presumable that some thought for the morrow must have crossed their minds. They cannot be supposed to be proposing a revolutionary alteration in the conditions governing the character of the relation between Britain and her Dependency merely for the sake of getting clear of a temporary difficulty such as a troublesome agitation. That would be to imagine ourselves back in the days when the first Irish Home Rule Bill, with all its consequences, was launched in a fit of impatience with obstruction in the Commons. No; we *must* have grown wiser since then; and therefore, when these Indian schemes make their appearance, we conclude that the authors have in view a self-governing India taking her place in the Imperial system something after the manner of South Africa, the new Government taking over the debt, obligations, and properties of its predecessor, with a minimum disturbance of vested interests—capital to remain secure in its investments, the private person free to pursue his industry or calling, the ports free to British trade, discarded British officials duly indemnified, and visible connection maintained by a Viceroy, and perhaps a few provincial Governors, with formal powers. All to go on as before except for the installation of an Indian Government working in general harmony with the ideas of Westminster—in short, a policy of association. The impediment, unfortunately, is that the conditions to be dealt with do not bear the smallest resemblance to those of South Africa or of any other Dominion. Some of the difficulties, or rather impossibilities, of finding any Government that will not glaringly misrepresent the masses of the people have been touched on above. We have now to look at the question from the Imperial point of view.

Owing to the preponderating importance of the public service, which in India is not only an executive, but the mainspring of all administrative progress, which is, in fact, the

best critic of the Government as well as its
agent—a condition which renders the introduction of any Parliamentary system subversive—the question of association inevitably
presents itself in a twofold aspect. Association in the public services is a matter distinct
from the political association that we assume
to be the aim of present-day reformers. The
former has been carried out to a considerable
extent already, and, as far as proposals go,
to the fullest extent compatible with the
maintenance of the existing system, in the
recommendations of the Public Services Commission. Nevertheless, as has been already
seen, the Commission's scheme has been
flouted everywhere as totally insufficient and
inadmissible. The Indian demand, with its
usual shrewdness, concentrates upon " Simultaneous Examinations," a watchword, outwardly specious, which would have the result
in the course of a few years of putting the
services entirely into Indian hands. To the
multitudes of the Indian colleges an appointment to one of the higher branches of the
public service is so great a prize that the
competition would be enormous, while to the
English candidate the inducement, much
smaller to start with, would shrink each year

as the Indian element increased until it
disappeared entirely. This may seem an
invidious assertion, but it is no more than
the expression of a fact, a fact which has
already come into evidence in the case of the
Indian Medical Service, which has for some
years been practically abandoned by the class
of candidates that were once forthcoming for
it. And at this point of the case we come
upon a set of considerations which are wisely
kept in the background when possible, but
which it is not possible to ignore. It is hard
to imagine political amalgamation as a success
where there is no social amalgamation; and
in spite of surface changes, English education, the frequency of visits to Europe, the
adoption by advanced Indians of European
manners of life, and the spread of the English
language; in spite, too, of much individual
goodwill on both sides, the gulf does not tend
to close, rather, perhaps, it widens.

Few men can have been so unfortunate as
to spend much time in the country without
contracting some close and valued friendships
with Indians, whose pleasant memories will
last through life; but in general intercourse
is restrained, as it must be between men
whose private lives are rigidly separated.

The most liberal-minded European shrinks
from being attended by an Indian doctor or
an Indian clergyman, and the idea of mixed
marriages excites on both sides a repugnance,
justified by the results that ensue when the
natural bar is disregarded. A certain distance
and scarcity of subjects of conversation
naturally follow, more noticeable to an
Englishman than to a Hindu, who does
not look for intimacy after our fashion
in his relations with men of his own race.
Belonging to a society which has added
to the barriers of caste the Mahomedan
institution of the zenana, the Hindu is not a
person easily known by anyone outside his
own circle. His religion, which enters into
all the acts of his life, is not so much a creed
as a social system, into which no outsider
can enter by virtue of subscribing to its
doctrines. To those who are born within the
fold all mankind is necessarily severed into
the two divisions, Hindu and non-Hindu, as
for the Israelites it was divided into Jew and
Gentile. But this people in whom the sense
of particularity is so strong has been endowed
in addition, unlike the Jew, and in contrast
with such races as the Armenian and the Parsi,
with an inflexible attachment to its own land.

With small powers of defence, but gifted with
an infinite patience, it has set itself to absorb
or sterilise the successive intruders into its
domain, after having made due use of them.
As it subdued its Mahomedan conquerors,
who nowadays must fall in behind or trust
to the sustaining power of the British Government, so it now turns instinctively to the
task of getting the upper hand of the foreign
Power of the moment. It would, of course,
be idle to think of a population of 220 millions
following out a reasoned policy, and equally
idle to suppose that it could be swayed by
any transient sentiments, gratitude for a concession or what not. Docile under authority,
if left to its own guidance it must go the
way its instincts take it, and there is nothing
to suggest that that way will take it in the
direction of assimilation.

The idea that India has only to be endowed
with self-government to complete the shining
circle of the Dominions ignores the vital fact
that the Dominions are Britain Overseas, and
that India can never come within that description. Because the Dominions are what they
are, essentially British in tone and temper,
the slenderness of the formal bond of connec-

tion is a matter of relatively small importance. Let us imagine, for instance, Australia so chagrined by the terms of the future peace in regard to the Bismarck Islands that she insisted on secession from the Empire. The retirement might very probably make no sensible difference. The same ideas as before would continue to prevail in both Governments, the same trade would continue to flow backwards and forwards, individuals would not diminish their intercourse nor their friendliness. But in India the introduction of self-government on the Colonial basis would bring changes much greater than a declaration of outright independence on the part of Australia or New Zealand. The ideas of the people are so different that the course of the country, if left to itself, would be centrifugal.

Even if the undisguised hostility of tone which runs through the utterances of the present political leaders were to be appeased by the surrender which in their memorials to Mr. Montagu and Lord Chelmsford they "demand," the conciliatory effect would be of the briefest duration. As has been pointed out above, all the effect of the Morley-Minto reforms has been to swell the agitation for more, in volume and in bitterness. Instead

of being a sedative, they have acted as an
irritant. Lord Morley thought that he was
embarking on a momentous change which
would make an impressive appeal to public
opinion when he admitted two Indians to
his Council. Now the demand is that this
Council, if continued, must consist at least
in half of Indian elected members, in addition
to whom the Secretary of State is to be assisted
by three Under-Secretaries all Indians. In
other words, the Indian politician does not
want an India Office at all; but if it is to
remain in existence, it must be an Office that
will bring no check to his plans. Where
these stop for the moment does not much
signify; a few years of Home Rule will bring
about surprising developments, and if the
experiment succeeded according to the Congress man's visions, and the Indian Parliamentary system did not end like the Persian,
forces would have been let loose that are
as yet only vaguely felt below the surface.
For instance, to begin with, every Indian in
the country is at heart a confirmed Protec-
tionist. If he is thinking of the town, he is
for octroi; if of the province, he would like
transit duties; if of the country at large, he
is for taxing the foreign importer to the hilt.

11

The whole of the Free-Trade policy he has had to put up with in conformity with the principles of Britain he has looked upon as a system, not of principles, but a giving away of advantages under the pressure of the dominant Power. One can easily judge how far such a people would be content to abide by any system set up for the rest of the Empire after they had had a Government of their own for a few years.

But in fact points on which collision would be bound to arise under any system of Home Rule abound on every side. The financial conscience is the weakest side usually of Indian public men, and in any case is it possible that a popular Government should go on for long without people beginning to question the amount of the obligations it has inherited ? The public debt: has not that been swollen by the faults of an extinct régime ? Pensions for the retired officers: is not that a matter for the country that sent them out ? And so on. The one conservative point in the reformers' programme is that the defence of the country shall be reserved to His Majesty's Government, the reason being perfectly intelligible. But if the British Army remains, causes of friction must remain. Supposing that the Hindu Parliament prohibits universally the killing of kine, which is the first measure a really popular Legislature in India would pass, who is to see that the soldiers get their beef ? Supposing a riot occurs, who is to call out the troops to suppress it ? Who is to ensure them fair trial afterwards ? If they do not get it, what is the commander to do ? It would be no answer to say, that these and similar matters were arranged for in the Act of Transfer. It would merely be said that the Treaty itself was wrong or obsolete. One may be told that the British Parliament could always intervene in the last resort; but the recovery of surrendered powers by the strong hand is a reversal of all ordinary experience. In the case of the Colonies we have seen the spirit of local self-management constantly growing; until in these days even the appearance of interfering in any question concerning their domestic politics is avoided as scrupulously as in the case of a foreign empire. The longer a separate Government in India endures, the more strenuously will any interference from outside be resisted. If this Government were likely to be British in spirit, it might keep direction with the rest of the Imperial band, while taking its own road. What we complain of in our reformers is that they have not paid the smallest attention to considering whether the spirit of association is there, and yet are thrusting to the front in panic haste a scheme which must miscarry on a vast scale if it is absent. Finally, no one, surely, will ask us to believe that when difficulties arise the Viceroy of the future on his Colonial footing will have any power to compose them. He is more likely to be submerged by difficulties of his own, for he will be confronted from the first with the constant prospect of having to choose between thwarting the desires of India or allowing measures to pass through his hands inconsistent with the intentions or interests of the King-Emperor's Government.

CHAPTER IX

No one likes to meet a scheme that comes forward decorated with the claims of a contribution to human progress, however elusive that idea may be, with a blank negative; and thus it is only natural that, as people have become more and more convinced by nearer consideration of the overwhelming objections to Indian reform on the lines laid down by Lord Morley and continued by Mr. Montagu, they should have turned to thoughts of circumventing the difficulty. Recent news from India shows that certain English non-officials and enlightened Indians have been taking counsel together for the contrivance of compromise schemes of representation; but as the proposed arrangements would seem to be artificial and elaborate, and as they are not the least likely to commend themselves to the Congress and the Moslem League, they need not be discussed here. A different line of advance, of a clearer, broader character,

153

which might supply an escape from the
threatened enthronement of an eclectic
oligarchy of lawyers and pedagogues in the
seat of power at Delhi, may be summed up
generally in the term decentralisation. This
long word may mean little or much, but the
ideas it adumbrates have been active since
the subject was stirred by a Royal Commission which, like the Public Services Commission, travelled up and down the country,
and was eventually delivered of an overgrown
report. Those who have read through this
ponderous production must be few indeed,
but in the meantime decentralisation had got
itself talked about, and everyone is by now
convinced that in the sense of giving more
freedom and initiative to the Local Governments it is the first administrative need of the
day. But from administrative reform we
may carry on the idea to political reform,
and Lord Islington, in a notable address
delivered at Oxford last year, gave clear
indications that he, for instance, had been
making this passage, and had been coming
out on conclusions not unlike those once made
familiar to the British public by the advocacy
of Mr. John Bright. The tide of events
ebbed away from the position where Mr.

Bright stood when the Government of India was passing into the hands of the Crown, but in recent days it has been flowing back, and were he alive now he might return to a cause which he ceased to press after he recognised that the tendencies of the times were contrary.

The first thing that anyone will notice who goes back to Mr. Bright's utterances on the subject is their complete unlikeness to those of our present leaders. He has no idea of concealing his hand, he never shrinks from stating his aim or from facing the ultimate effects of his proposals. If he thought that he had it within his reach to confer a good upon the people, he would have poured contempt on the idea of giving them a glimpse of it and then telling them that they must await the bestowal for some geological period. Mr. Bright took his stand on the position that the British occupation of India must be a transitory phenomenon in history. Fifty or one hundred or five hundred years it might last, but the end must come of such an unnatural connection, and it was our business to leave something behind that would endure of itself after us. The grand defects he saw in the British system proceeded from the centralised character of the Government, and, above all, in the concentrated power of the Governor-General. As a Quaker he hated war; that the chronicles of British India from 1800 to 1858 had been a story of wars was undeniable, and for this he was disposed to lay the blame on the personal ambitions of successive Governor-Generals. On other grounds, moreover, he considered the office a stumbling-block. " I believe," he said, " the duties of the Governor-General are far greater than any human being can adequately fulfil. He has a power omnipotent to crush everything that is good. If he so wishes, he can overrule and overbear anything that is proposed for the welfare of India; while as to anything that is good, I could show, with regard to the vast territories over which he rules, he is really almost powerless to effect anything which these countries require. . . . I do not know at this moment, and I have never known, a man competent to govern India, and if any man says he is competent he sets himself at a much higher value than those who know him are likely to set him." Then Mr. Bright went on to his own remedy. " I propose that instead of a Governor-General and an Indian Empire we should have neither the one nor the other. I propose that we should have Presidencies, and not an Empire."

The expression "these countries" will have been noticed in the above sentences, as coming from a man who never used language at random. It was a deep sense of the diversity of India that led Bright into revolt against the British Indian system. Much more would he have scouted the notion of handing on the same scheme of government to Indians. It was, in fact, just because he was looking for something better that he was brought to his separate Presidency system. As usual, he is explicit enough about this: "Does any man with the smallest glimmering of common sense believe that so great a country, with its twenty different nations and its twenty languages, can ever be consolidated into one compact Empire? I believe such a thing to be totally impossible. We must fail in the attempt if we make it, and we are bound to look into the future with reference to that point." "Under the Presidency system," he goes on, "if it were to continue for a century or more, there would be five or six Presidencies built up into so many compact States; and if the sovereignty

of England should be withdrawn, we should
have so many Presidencies, each able to
support its own independence," instead of
" leaving the country a prey to that discord
and anarchy which I believe to be inevitable
if we insist on holding these vast territories
with the idea of building them up into one
vast Empire."

Things have come round within these last
days with startling rapidity into a situation
which brings Mr. Bright's concernments with
the future into relation with practical politics.
The withdrawal from India is coming into
plain view as the logical consequence of the
schemes of politicians who, unlike him, instead
of frankly disclosing their ultimate purpose,
do their best to hide it like a guilty secret.
The question before us is whether Mr. Bright's
scheme of provincial Home Rule offers any
refuge from the glaring faults of the Home
Rule of to-day. Alas ! it is too soon found
to be beset with equal objections. It will
have been seen that the first condition of
his plan is the disappearance of the Government of India and Governor-General, and the
substitution of some half-dozen Presidencies,
each knowing only in the last resort the

paramount control of the Secretary of State. These Provincial Administrations are to be of equal status, each with its own Governor, its own Council and Legislature, and its own army. And each, of course, was to raise and spend its own revenues. But the first objection is that it is not possible to make out of the major Provinces of India a group of independent States in any sort resembling, for instance, the Australian Colonies, with their general similarity of circumstances, each with its own seaboard and an unlimited stretch of waste hinterland at its back.

Under any scheme of the kind the Punjab would have to bear three-fourths of the burden of defence for the entire country, though it would have no sea-coast, no foreign trade, and no customs revenue; while rich Provinces like Bengal and Madras would have the trade and revenue, but would be free of the burdens of defence. It is true that Mr. Bright contemplated that each of the States should maintain its own provincial army; but where would be the incentive for the raising of an effective army of Bengalis, representing so much superfluous cost and effort, on the hypothesis that the scheme worked smoothly ? If, on the other hand, as is tolerably certain, human nature being what it is, the Northern Provinces, after a few years, should refuse to put up with their disadvantageous position and begin asserting their superior physical force to amend it, as they used to do of yore, there would be an end of the provincial system, and we should be faced with the choice of renewed British intervention or a relapse into the chaos that followed on the decline of the Moghul.

But apart from this, no one less resolute, and, it may be said without disrespect, less prejudiced, than Mr. Bright could contemplate getting rid of all vestige of a central authority in India. If collections of States so homogeneous as the Australian Colonies have been forced to federate for the better management of their common affairs, it is clear that States made up of various races, separated by almost all the differences that can divide men, with a long tradition of past hostilities into the bargain, could not set up in business at all under the system in contemplation without having contrived some form of central Government. It is impossible to conceive a condition of things under which it would be open to the Government of Bengal, offended, say, by some quarrel between the Allahabad and Calcutta Universities, to seek satisfaction by shutting out sea-borne imports from the United Provinces. Matters, then, such as customs, internal trade (whose importance in a great territorial country English people are apt to overlook), the railways, the posts and telegraphs, the currency and coinage, must be placed under the regulation of some common authority, which, moreover, will require to be furnished with the power to enforce its decrees. An Australian or an American, however much he may detest particular acts of the Federal Government, does not dream of repudiating it, because at its worst it is his Government. But a newly constituted Federal Government in India would in its relations with the Provinces have no moral force whatever behind it, and if it is to be effective must lean on some external support. Again we come back to unhappy Britain, which, after having surrendered all the advantages of the connection, is still found saddled with all the invidious responsibilities.

It may be said, perhaps, that it is a waste of time to follow up to their consequences extravagant notions entertained by no person of sober judgment; but there are many views

in active circulation at the present moment
that are not particularly marked by sobriety,
and when the idea of an early British withdrawal is indisputably in vogue, it is worth
while to point out by how many roads we
arrive at some barrier to that simple settlement.   But supposing for the sake of argument the big questions relating to the retirement of the British power comfortably
disposed of, let us take the case of one of the
new quasi-autonomous Provinces started in
life on its own account with an Administration
of the type prescribed by Indian politicians
—that is to say, an Executive Council of
four or five members, headed, to begin with,
· by a *fainéant* English Governor, and an
elected Legislative Council which cannot turn
out this Executive, but which can criticise
and rebuke it, alter its budgets, pass the laws
which it must enforce, and dictate by means
of resolutions the policy it must follow.
Obviously, in no long time all power must pass
into the hands of the second body, and the
question is—accepting the democratic principle—what is the prospect that it will represent the people as a whole ?

Now, Mr. Bright took as the model of his
Presidencies the Province of Madras.   He

considered it as geographically the most compact unit, and the most adaptable generally for the purposes of his scheme. It is at this day in some respects the most advanced Province in India. But if we look at the population of Madras, we come upon a diversity as various as can be found in any other portion of India. The great mass of the people are of the Dravidian race, Tamils and Telugus, speaking their own languages, as different from Hindi as from Latin. Then there are 6,755,000 who speak Malayalam, and 1,600,000 speaking Canarese. The unity of the Province consists in religion, 87 per cent. of the whole population being Hindus. Socially, however, and politically religion is no bond, for the Brahman or the Nair have no more in common with the Hindu Tamil coolie than with the lowly Christians of the Madras bazaar. These inferior multitudes probably do not feel it as any grievance that the Brahmans have a practical monopoly of the places in the public service, employment to which they can scarcely aspire. But a political ascendancy would be a different matter, for it would mean that they would be taxed and managed exclusively in the interests of those above them. To some extent this has lately been borne in upon them, and, as well as they can, they have been manifesting their objections to reform. The British democrat may say that, being a great majority, they have the remedy in their own hands. Why not a Tamil party, a Peasants' League, an Indian Christian Association ? The answer is that no one who knows these people can contemplate a franchise extending to the masses. The political classes themselves would oppose any such proposal strenuously, and they would be right.

One consideration more. Provincial autonomy in any shape has the defect that it would not, as a policy, in the least appeal to the class whom we are striving to satisfy. All their aim, on the contrary, is to obscure and get out of sight the existence of any differences of whatsoever kind between Indians. Whenever we hear them speaking, it is of the Indian nation, the Indian opinion of a subject, Indian aspirations and Indian demands. Their great object is to get the outer world to forget the differences between a Beloochi and a Babu, and so to accept them on their own presentation as the people of India. They are clever tacticians who know the value of reiteration, but those who are taken in by the artifice must be those who are determined to be deluded.

The idea of autonomous Provinces cannot, moreover, be considered without reference to the existence of the Native States. These principalities collectively cover an area of over 700,000 square miles, as against the million square miles of British India, with a population of 70 odd millions against the 315 millions of the British territories. They have fallen into their places with wonderful loyalty in the general scheme of the Indian Empire under the Crown, but how would it be when the common tie that binds them in allegiance to the Sovereign was removed and they found themselves the next-door neighbours of provincial republics with no claim upon their deference ? The dominions of the Nizam, even without the Province of Berar, are about the same size as Behar and Orissa, and rather larger than the new Bengal. Kashmir is even larger than Hyderabad territorially. The extent of the Central India Agency, into which comes the great State of Gwalior, is more than that of Bombay without Sind and little less than that of Bengal. In the day when Mr. Bright advocated his

separate Provinces, all the Chiefs had armies
of some sort, and some of them large armies.
If the Government of India had on his advice
been abolished there and then, the military
predominance would have passed to the
Nizam and the Maharaja Sindhia, who would
have been left with the most powerful armies
in the country; and if the new Provincial
Governments had preserved good terms with
these Chiefs, they would have had to acknowledge the situation by a considerable show of
deference.   The change that has taken place
in the States and their rulers during the last
three or four decades is quite as great as any
change that can be pointed to in British
India.   The Chiefs, when the writer first
knew the country, were intensely suspicious
of each other, jealous of their gradations of
rank, and their only social intercourse was
when they happened to meet at a Durbar.
Now they have become a select society of
friends, united, many of them, by the memories
of past days at the Mayo College or in the
Cadet Corps, and even the announcement that
a Hindu Raja has been paying a friendly
visit to a neighbouring Nawab rouses no
astonishment.

The Administration has changed as much

as the rulers.   Formerly it was often easy to
tell that one had crossed the border of a
Native State from the mere appearance of
the country and people.   Nowadays the
visitor to such places as Jeypore, Gwalior,
Mysore, and many others, with their architectural beauties, their modern institutions, the
high standard of order, comfort, and content-
ment observable on every hand, and maintained without friction, comes away with the
feeling that he has seen India at its best and
happiest, and many have said it.   I am not
writing to suggest that there is an imperative
need for revolutionary departures in any
shape, but if we are invited to consider the
case for British withdrawal from the country,
we might surely, while we are about changing
the foundations of rule, take account of the
alternative reconstruction available in the
form of making over the country to a Federa-
tion of Native States.   The idea is, of course,
beset with abundant objections, but it is not
more impracticable than self-government with
representative institutions to be worked by
men who have not the vestige of a democratic
conviction in their compositions, and we
should at any rate be starting the new order
with a form of government comprehended by
the people.

CHAPTER X

ON THE VERGE OF THE PRECIPICE

IF there is any truth in the exposition presented in the foregoing chapters, the reader will have come to discern that we have arrived in India at a situation to which there is no parallel. A Government with a record of admitted success and continuous improvement, strong and powerful, popular with the masses of its subjects, and looked up to by them as an embodiment of rectitude and impartiality, is on the point of being manœuvred out of its seat of power by a newly grown clan of men who have made none of the exertions and endured none of the sacrifices that Liberty requires of her suitors before she is won. Their pretensions are not backed by the masses of their countrymen, but they impose them on the outer world by a borrowed Western vocabulary and a surface enthusiasm for Western political ideas. The strength of this movement lies, not within itself, but in the sympathy, or, it would be

truer to say, in the indifference, of the British
democracy. "They seem to be making a
great rumpus about self-government; if self-
government will satisfy the beggars, why not
let 'em have it ?"—that seems to be the
attitude of a great number of our homely
politicians. But deeper than this, of course,
is the feeling that the changes foreshadowed
by Mr. Montagu are democratic—that is to
say, progressive, elevating, virtuous; and
then still deeper down is the strange fatalistic
idea that any democratic proposal, once
launched, must go on to its accomplishment.
How often in this connection does one hear
the expression "There can be no going back,"
a proposition that no one would accept in
private life if he saw himself making for a
precipice, but is often accepted as closing the
question. If India was in the condition to-day
of England in 1830, in a state of fierce and
general agitation for political reform, it would
be another matter; but the discontent and
sedition that are abroad are not founded on a
desire for political reform, and the political
leaders with whom we are dealing have even
now no control over the would-be revolution-
aries. Their aim, if they do not formulate
it, is simply to attain a position from which

they can lay hold of the revenue raised from
the masses for the benefit of the middle class,
free education, an octopus bureaucracy, inter-
minable litigation, and the like.   It is a perfectly intelligible ambition, but it is hardly
the business of the British democrat to pro-
mote it.

Wherever the successes of democracy in
Britain may lie, it is hard to discover its
virtues in that field of British responsibilities
which is represented by the Indian Empire.
It used to be commonly said at the time when
the Crown was taking over the Government
that now would be seen a great increase of
public interest and Parliamentary interest in
the affairs of India.   People feared, in fact,
that the interest might be excessive, and that
the House of Commons busybodies would by
incessant criticism and inquisitiveness exert a
warping influence over the Secretary of State.
These expectations have turned out on a par
with the prophecies so often heard on the
laying of a new cable or the launching of a new
steamer, that the two countries are evidently
approaching to the day when closer intercourse will bring better social understanding,
and in fulness of time social fusion.   In point

of fact, Parliament has never been so much occupied with India as it was in the decade 1773-1783, when the virulent charges made against Clive during the passage of Lord North's Regulating Act drove the founder of British India into melancholia and suicide, and when the King threw himself into the fray to defeat the India Bill of Mr. Fox, and thus paved the way for the rise of Mr. Pitt. A return to the excitements of those days might be a serious matter now, with an educated Indian public waiting for the reports at the other end of the cable; but it is evident that no such revival need be apprehended. The interest of the House of Commons in India has shrunk *pari passu* with the advance of democracy, until even the annual discussion of the Indian Budget seems to have been quietly allowed to lapse. If the House of Lords were now to be abolished, India as a Parliamentary interest would be extinct. This indifference, which casts all care upon the Secretary of State, leaving him, or rather asking him, to pursue his own way, be it bad or good, as long as the ruling country is not troubled with the unwelcome subject, is a strange manifestation as the eventual outcome of all that we are accustomed to hear of the merits and the tendencies of popular government.

A singular phenomenon to those who have feared that the besetting sin of democracy in dealing with distant possessions would be an excessive interference in details, hampering the power of the Executive and sapping its sense of responsibility, must be the situation now before our eyes in India, where a couple of worthy gentlemen of no commanding reputation and little experience have assumed a free hand to settle questions that would tax the highest statesmanship. And more than this, they have not only obtained in advance the support of the present Government for whatever settlement they may arrive at, but have pledged any succeeding Government to persevere and follow a policy, even though it is still undisclosed. The pledge is of no validity, for it is axiomatic that no Government, much less a single Minister out on the loose, can bind its successors; but it will make the difficulty of going back upon a decision additionally formidable. In any case, that two persons, having obtained the connivance of the Cabinet, should be left to fashion out an undertaking of such consequence to the Empire at their own will and discretion is a remarkable illustration of the effectuality of government by the many when it comes to practical working.

⁎ In truth, the constant lip-homage to democracy as a good in itself, which is nothing more than flattery addressed to the multitude by those whom the system has brought to the top, is an unwholesome symptom of the times. Though freedom of opinion suffers in these days under a sense of discouragement, men have been found bold to aver that democracy is on its trial; and without going to that stretch of audacity, it may be said that most thoughtful persons have come to recognise that it is not democracy that brings about a good social state; but that it is where it finds a good social soil to start upon that the democratic system of polity takes root and flourishes and puts forth fruit abundantly. The United States furnishes the world with the best example of the latter conditions; but, on the other hand, in Turkey, in Persia, in China, and, last of all, in Russia, we have surely had recent and melancholy examples enough of the fact that a change in the form of government and the adoption of nominally representative institutions can do nothing to remedy diseased

social conditions, or to restore a declining
national constitution, or to create a public
spirit that is absent. The introduction of
representative institutions into India as the
governing principle, with Home Rule for the
goal and the disappearance of the British
element at the different stages along the road,
would not follow the same course as events
have taken in Persia or Petrograd, since
democracy is a cult that each nation modifies
as it receives it according to its own qualities
or deficiencies. What the Hindus would
eventually make of it is a mere speculation,
but there is not an element present in the
conditions of the experiment to encourage a
belief that the outcome could be answerable
to the hopes of its British authors. For the
Indian agitation, as is implied even by its
latest exponents, is not for Home Rule proper,
but for the rule by an eclectic class of a
country to be held down by British bayonets
while they have their way of it—a conception
altogether new to political reformers.

As we near the conclusion, the writer
anticipates the criticism that he has not
disclosed any plan of his own. The answer is
that it would require considerable self-confi-
dence on the part of any single person to

suppose that he had any plan for dealing with such a situation as that which has been brought about in India. The object of these pages has been to show how serious the position is, and to awaken those who may read them to the very real danger that the British public may find that, while its attention has been turned elsewhere, it has been committed by hasty agents to changes that may lead up to nothing less than the loss of its Indian Empire, or to the necessity of the reassertion of British authority with a stronger hand. It has been shown, to the best of the writer's competence, that a Home Rule settlement established, with however specious an equipment of representative institutions, must fail, because in the social conditions of the country there is no basis for such a political edifice, and because the class that would monopolise the working of the new system would have no physical power to enforce its own rule. Conscious of this, the most advanced of the agitators couple with their demands the condition that Britain shall retain the business of defence; in other words, that the British Army shall remain and the British Navy continue to be responsible for the protection of Indian trade.

What are the earliest consequences to be expected of this parody of Home Rule ? The peasantry, vaguely aware of a general relaxation in the authority of the Government, and catching some of the excitement of the political hubbub, breaks out into agrarian risings after the manner of the late tumults in Behar, but on a vastly larger and more formidable scale. No one can, in fact, calculate the extent to which such ferments might not spread when the restraining influence of the British District Officer and his handful of assistants had been withdrawn. But the army is still there, and is now called upon by the new Government to restore order. So that the next step in the process is that our forces are brought upon the scene to crush and quell our late subjects and friends, the ryots, for the sake of the politicals. The impossibility of setting up a Government which has not the power of sustaining itself leads, indeed, to consequences absurd in contemplation, ruinous if they should come to reality. The ethical aspects of the position have been set forth by Froude in a passage so apposite to the present case that I cannot forbear to quote it here :

The right of a people to self-government, says the historian, consists, and can consist, in nothing but their power to defend themselves. . . . There is no freedom possible to men except in obedience to law : and those who, cannot prescribe a law to themselves, if they desire to be free, must be content to accept direction from others. The right to resist depends upon the power of resistance. But when resistance has been tried and has failed, when the inequality has been proved beyond dispute, the wisdom, and ultimately the duty, of the weaker party is to accept the benefits which are offered in return for submission; and a nation which will not defend its liberties in the field, nor yet allow itself to be governed, yet struggles to preserve the independence which it wants the spirit to uphold in arms by insubordination and anarchy and secret crime, may bewail its wrongs in wild and weeping eloquence in the ears of mankind—may at length, in a time when the methods by which sterner ages repressed that kind of conduct are unpermitted, make itself so intolerable as to be cast off and bidden to go its own bad way; but it will not go for its own benefit. It will have established no principle and vindicated no natural right: liberty only profits those who can govern themselves better than others can govern them, and those who are able to govern themselves wisely have no reason to petition for a privilege they can take or keep for themselves.

The sentences occur at the beginning of Froude's work on Ireland. But even the miscarriage of Home Rule in Ireland would be a small matter as regards the general consequences in comparison with the miscarriage of Home Rule in India.

Yet, it will be said, expectations have been raised which cannot be blankly negatived. You cannot expect Mr. Montagu to return from his "epoch-making" mission with the confession that he has been able to achieve nothing. It may be submitted that Mr. Montagu's personal reputation does not concern the world at large; but undoubtedly the situation he has gratuitously brought to a climax does present us with the prospect of a violent and troublesome agitation if the promise of self-government should be suddenly withdrawn. On the other hand, it is true that those who have held out to political India the promise of emancipation have continually coupled this with qualifications as to the generations that the process must require, and with exhortations as to the need of abundant patience before the fruit can drop. This part of the discourse is seldom well received, and it is perfectly certain that no tinkering reforms will be of the least avail as a remedy for discontent and disaffection. Like the Morley-Minto measures, they will merely swell the outcry. The patience that we ask of the Indians might possibly be employed to better effect by ourselves in simply facing the present outcry, and determining to go on in the exercise of that authority which Britain cannot really resign, on the principles of justice, impartiality, and a paramount concern for the general welfare of the people. It is more than possible that if this intention could be clearly understood agitation would subside, and the classes now against us, because they believe us to be wavering, would be more disposed to take their own place in the system. But, of course, the difficulties of setting up any declaration of policy that would be accepted as binding are great, because of the uncertain attitude of the British electorate. All that can be said is that if that public cannot be brought to distinguish the shadow from the substance, if they persist in believing the people of Hindustan to be oppressed and unhappy in the absence of forms of government completely similar to their own, the old question of whether a democracy can be capable of ruling a dependency will have been answered in the negative.

Confronted, however, as he has been, by the evidence of the emphatic objections to his policy of benevolence entertained by large communities on the spot, the likelihood seems to be that Mr. Montagu will endeavour to temporise with some scheme which shall combine the appearance of large concessions with the provision of a more or less elaborate system of checks. No expedient on those lines, if the checks are to be effective, will appease the agitators, who are quicksighted enough in these matters, and the reform will be merely a starting-point for a fresh campaign against the remaining restraints. The difficulty of our reformers, whether in Simla or the India Office, seems to come largely from their persistence in regarding the country as a single administrative unit. Decentralisation may be on their lips, but their hearts are far from it. Every tax, every duty, every policy that is announced by " Resolution " is issued for the whole country indiscriminately, when the circumstances of different Provinces and the character of their populations may vary as much as those of Belgium and East Prussia.

Allowing that as a political system the idea
of autonomous Presidencies with no connect-
ing central organisation, Mr. Bright's idea,
is an impossibility, is it necessary to keep
perpetually to the other extreme ?   A great
opportunity was palpably lost when the reform
of the Legislative Councils was taken in hand.
There was no need that the new system should
have been imposed on the whole country at
one stroke, when it might have been introduced in one or two Provinces to start with,
and the working of the experiment watched.
But in any case, it should have been confined
to the Provinces in the first instance, and
the Viceroy's Legislative Council left as it
stood.   The Provincial Legislatures deal with
business at first hand, and their non-official
members, as men acquainted with the people
and country, can and do bring on occasion
useful help and criticism.   The Viceroy's
Council stands on quite a different footing,
and there was no necessity for change.   Had
it been allowed to remain as it was, the
European element, through the nominated
members, would have continued to enjoy a
fair representation, and one glaring anomaly
in the present situation would have been
avoided.   As it is, the Imperial Legislative

13

Council, while it has eclipsed the others politically, consists of a collection of persons supposed to represent different selected interests in different parts of the country, whose coming together in one Chamber has merely helped to create that artificial appearance of unity that is responsible for so much error and mischief. The mistake once made, in face of better advice, cannot be repaired, but it is submitted that if compromises are in quest, the best way if the Councils are to be converted into Parliaments would be to commence with one or two Provinces, leaving the Viceregal Council severely alone on its present footing. If this were coupled with the exclusion of Calcutta and Bombay as separate enclaves somewhat on the model of the Delhi territory, which the Government of India reserves to itself, so as to secure the great European interests in those centres, a start might be made with Bombay and Bengal. There would be difficulties, of course, plenty of them, but the plan might offer an escape from the wholesale plunge into self-government, with all its dark possibilities.

Then as to the policy of association. Here, again, if anything is to be done, it must be by striking out on new lines. We must escape

altogether out of the hackneyed path of the
Civil Service Commissioners, and the Indian
Education Department, and the Public
Services Commission. Experience has proved
with dismal certainty that the young Hindu
who passes for the Civil Service, however
good his essay on the predecessors of Dryden,
or however much he may have assimilated
the marginal theorem in economic analysis,
is not a success as an associate. The Hindu
matures early, and these young men who
come over from the Indian colleges to enter
at Oxford and Cambridge, or to study law
and medicine, have already lost the openness
and pliancy of boyhood. They keep to themselves in their own colonies, acquire little
touch with European life, and are, quite
intelligibly, apt to resent well-meant intru-
sion in the feeling of the Greek saw, "Don't
try to live in my mind." It is common
knowledge that there are none in India so
anti-English as those who have been educated
in England. The two prime plotters of anarchist crime—Hurdyal and Krishnavarma—
were both men who did notably well at Oxford.
Is it not plain that, if the aim is to anglicise
the Indian to good purpose, there must be a
total change of system; he must be caught

young, at the age when the Admiralty catches
its boys for the Navy? Then, with five
years at a public school, there would be a
chance of turning him out an Englishman in
spirit, and at any rate with some firmly
rooted English friendships and a stock of
wholesome English associations that would
be an influence through life. Of course, the
parents of the boys who surrendered them
at this early age would require some sort of
guarantee as to their future prospects; also,
they would have to be selected parents of
means and respectable position, and all this
would involve a recasting of the present
system and a break with the Civil Service
Commissioners. But, after all, is not anything better than stolid persistence in the
way of assured failure?

But there appears to be no reason why the
system indicated should stop short at the
candidates for the public services. A certain
number of expensive State scholarships, more
really in the nature of travelling fellowships,
are given to Indians to enable them to get a
technical training in European factories and
workshops. In nine cases out of ten, nothing
seems to come of it. The literary young man
keeps to the bookwork of the business, and

eventually emerges into the world as uncertain
of finding his footing in it as when he started.
If instead of one scholar we took twenty
boys, say, of the weaver caste, and apprenticed
them to Lancashire cotton-mills, there would
be a chance that some of them would turn
the experience to good account for themselves and for their country, and so with the
other trades hereditarily followed in India.
Again, we build in India a model Agricultural
College with the idea of infusing the science
of the subject among the landowning classes
and their connections. But a college that
does not lead to appointments has no attractions for the middle-class student, and the
institution remains empty. Much, again,
might possibly be done by getting hold of
young boys of the agricultural classes, placing
them with cottagers in England, and letting
them take their education at the village school
while they learnt farming under a farmer.
These boys, taken from the hardier classes,
would be unencumbered with the besetting
Indian notion of the indignity of labour.
They would grow up in the habit of making
themselves useful, and by the time they were
twenty-one might be fine fellows and good
citizens to boot. The trouble would be that

most of them might decline to return, but those who did would be worth something to their native land.

These suggestions may labour under the imputation of being of a speculative cast, whereas the ways we have adopted have nothing against them but proved failure. But however that may be, the principle contended for has become a matter of the first practical importance in the case of the army, now that the King's commission has been formally opened to Indians. For a time, no doubt, all the available places will be required to meet the claims of Native officers who have done conspicuous service during the present war. But in fulness of time the question of direct appointment will come up, and it is one that deserves to be weighed beforehand.

The first consideration is that the new element should not break up the life of the regimental mess, which in India especially is the officer's home, and this, again, requires that the Native officers who are brought in must be men completely anglicised. An occasional promotion from the lower grades, being probably a man of the right sort, can get along well enough; but when direct appointments become systematic the only chance of avoiding failure lies in social fusion, for which it is necessary that the Indian officer should become as his fellows. I believe it was His Royal Highness the Duke of Connaught who, when the question of commissions was ventilated many years ago, suggested the establishment of an Indian Sandhurst. The proposal, suitable enough for the time when it was advanced, would seem to be out of the question now. If such a military college educating young men did not become a hunting ground for agitators in every capacity from the Professors down to the table servants,* the cadets would, some of them at any rate, be exposed to sinister influences before joining, in the vacations, and after leaving college. But if the Indian officer is to be worth his place, he must not be a doubtful quantity. Again, to give him a fair chance he must be caught young—educated preferably at a British public school, and on discharge from Sandhurst or Woolwich gazetted, not to an

---

* This is no extravagant supposition. In one of the criminal conspiracy trials it came out that a determined anarchist had wormed his way as a tutor into the household of the foremost of Indian loyalists, Maharaja Sir Pertab Singh of Jodpore.

Indian, but to a British corps. After three or four years with a British regiment, in addition to previous training, you would have a man thoroughly steeped in the spirit and tradition of the service, capable of taking his place without effort amongst his fellows, and beyond temptation to a relapse. The material is there if it is properly selected and properly utilised.

There is a certain sense of futility, however, in the discussion of suggestions of improvement or palliatives while the main question remains unsettled—namely, whose is to be the rule? A singular situation it would be if the British power in India, which has outridden so many emergencies, which before it was securely established found itself confronted by the ambitions of Bonaparte, which within present memories was cheerfully bracing itself to meet the apparently inevitable onset of the Muscovite—if this power should be discovered to have been surrendered away in a fit of national absent-mindedness. It will be useless in that case to lay the blame on the political genius of Lord Chelmsford, or on the personal ascendancy of Mr. Montagu, for the fault will lie with the indifference of the British public. As a last word one might entreat that public to dismiss for once confused politico-moral ideas as to natural rights, self-determination, and what not, and to look at the matter from the point of view of its own interests, which have their own clear claim to consideration. For if there is any validity in the arguments that have been advanced in the preceding pages, they lead with uncompromising distinctness to the conclusion that the step now being thrust upon us, however much its nature may be concealed by wrapping it up in the current phrases of everyday political controversy, must in reality be a decisive one. We have under our eyes in Ireland an example of how the concession of Parliamentary Home Rule has given birth to a fierce agitation for complete independence and severance, even before the new system has come into operation. How is it to be imagined that we can set up any half-way house for India ? Can it be supposed for a moment that a huge and distant country, with its millions of Asiatics who have only the vaguest notions of the land which claims their allegiance, will maintain its placid course along the road we have staked out for it, in due observance of the constitutional rules, checks, and conventions prescribed to preserve the connection and to secure the interests of the Imperial power after the exercise of effectual authority has been resigned ? The idea goes clean contrary to all probability and 'experience. India cannot serve two masters, and if Britain stands aside she will have to cleave to the men on the spot. She will not like it, but the election will not be hers, it will have been forced upon her by the people of England, who therefore should surely weigh well the consequences of the innocent-looking step that they are invited to take. That they are indifferent to the subject can scarcely be believed, seeing that the preservation of India against the Russian menace was the pivoting point of our foreign policy from the middle of the nineteenth century to its close, seeing even at the present moment what costly and distracting efforts are imposed upon Britain's sorely taxed energies by the necessity of preserving her dominion in Asia. What other meaning has the campaign in Mesopotamia except that of a precaution to keep the enemy's influence at a safe distance from India? It would seem, therefore, that after all we are very much of the same conviction as those before us who

judged that no sacrifice or exertion or personal hazard was too great if they helped
their country to win this great prize and to
hold it against the envy of the world.   But if
in these last days the democratic mind has
become insensible to the appeal of national
prestige, the merely material consequences
that would follow to every household in the
country from allowing India to slip out of our
keeping should be well appreciated.   They
cannot, of course, be tabled out in advance,
but their general effect could not fail to be
immense.

Considering the array of vested interests
involved, the capital sunk, the numbers
dependent on its returns, the importance
of Indian products to British industry,
the numbers of British employed in the
country either officially or commercially,
the army of persons on this side—merchants, shippers, distributors, producers, and
consumers—whose prosperity and conveni-
ence are more or less bound up with the
Indian connection, is it not plain that the
effect upon them, and by consequence upon
the whole people of this country, of any
rupture of the tie would amount to a social
disaster of the first magnitude ?   The instal-

ment of a Hindu Government in India, whether it led up to internal chaos or to internal passivity with exclusiveness against the outer world, would in fact be the beginning of a revolution in the material condition of the English people.

BILLING AND SONS, LTD., PRINTERS. GUILDFORD, ENGLAND

Lightning Source UK Ltd.
Milton Keynes UK
UKHW021219040422
401067UK00006B/915